THE PAST IN

Series Editors: C. C. Eldridge and Ralph A. Griffiths

DISRAELI AND THE RISE OF A NEW IMPERIALISM

THE PAST IN PERSPECTIVE

Series Editors: C. C. Eldridge and Ralph A. Griffiths

C. C. Eldridge is Reader in History at the University of Wales, Lampeter.

Ralph A. Griffiths is Professor of Medieval History at the University of Wales, Swansea.

Other titles in this series:

Revolution in Religion: The English Reformation, 1530–1570
David Loades

Protestant Dissenters in Wales, 1639–1689
Geraint H. Jenkins

Revolution in America: Britain and the Colonies, 1763–1776
Peter D. G. Thomas

The Road to 1789: From Reform to Revolution in France
Nora Temple

Ireland Divided: The Roots of the Modern Irish Problem
Michael Hughes

THE PAST IN PERSPECTIVE

DISRAELI AND THE RISE OF A NEW IMPERIALISM

C. C. Eldridge

CARDIFF
UNIVERSITY OF WALES PRESS
1996

British Library Cataloguing-In-Publication Data.
A catalogue record for this book is available from the British
Library.

ISBN 0-7083-1352-3

Typeset at the University of Wales Press
Printed in Great Britain by Dinefwr Press, Llandybïe

Contents

Editors' Foreword

Each volume in this series, *The Past in Perspective*, deals with a major theme of British, European or World history. The aim of the series is to engage the interest of all for whom knowledge of the riches of the world's historical experience is a delight, and in particular to meet the needs of students of history in universities and colleges — and at comparatively modest cost.

Each theme is tackled at sufficient length and in sufficient depth to allow each writer both to advance our understanding of the subject in the light of the most recent research, and to place his or her approach in due perspective. Accordingly, each volume contains a historiographical chapter which assesses how interpretations of its theme have developed, and have been criticized, endorsed, modified or discarded. Each volume, too, includes a section of substantial excerpts from key original sources: this reflects the importance of allowing the reader to come to his or her own conclusions about differing interpretations, and also the greater accessibility nowadays of original sources in print. Furthermore, in each volume there is a detailed bibliography which not only underpins the writer's own account and analysis, but also enables the reader to pursue the theme, or particular aspects of it, to even greater depth; the explosion of historical writing in the twentieth century makes such guidance invaluable. By these perspectives, taken together, each volume is an up-to-date, authoritative and substantial exploration of themes, ancient, medieval and modern, of British, European, American and World significance, after more than a century of the study and teaching of history.

C. C. Eldridge and Ralph A. Griffiths

Explanatory note
Reference to the Illustrative Documents which follow the main text

are indicated by a bold roman numeral preceded by the word 'DOCUMENT', all within square brackets [**DOCUMENT XII**].

The author wishes to acknowledge the kind permission of the editorial board of *Trivium* to use material previously published in that journal.

1. Prophet or Charlatan?

On 11 March 1880, *The Times* claimed that the word 'imperialism' had been invented to stamp Lord Beaconsfield's supposed designs with disapproval. There was some truth in the statement. The term had a longer history, dating back to the 1840s, when it was first used to describe the desire of *le parti impérialiste* in France to revive the glories of the Napoleonic era. Its first use in British domestic politics occurred in 1876 during heated arguments about creating Queen Victoria 'Empress of India'. Disraeli's subsequent actions in foreign and imperial affairs, especially his conduct of the Eastern Question, caused further controversy. By the general election of 1880, 'imperialism', and Gladstone's popular variant, 'Beaconsfieldism', had become political smear-words.

Another new word, 'jingoism', had also been coined. All three related to Disraeli's controversial foreign and imperial policies and their impact on Britain. Gladstone's indictment of these developments in his Midlothian campaigns of 1879–80 achieved a spectacular success at the hustings. Subsequently, however, following Gladstone's much criticized failures in the foreign and imperial fields during his ministry of 1880–5, Disraeli's reputation acquired a new glitter and a legend of his imperial vision began to grow. His name became associated with the reawakening of an expansionist imperial spirit in the late nineteenth century and with the coming of the 'New Imperialism'.

This book examines not simply the older controversies concerning Disraeli's attitude to colonies prior to 1866 (when he was allegedly a 'Little Englander' or anti-imperialist), the significance of his Crystal Palace speech in 1872 (which supposedly forged the link between the empire and the Conservative party), and his foreign and imperial policies of 1874–80 which caused so much controversy. It also discusses more recent claims that Disraeli was responsible for beginning the New Imperialism with his Abyssinian expedition of 1867–8, and that he contributed, in his second ministry (1874–80), a new facet to the character of British imperialism — an unashamed, militant and illiberal spirit that glorified the achievements of British rule overseas — which remained part of the national outlook into the twentieth century. By examining Disraeli's ideas and policies in their domestic, foreign and imperial contexts, this book is designed to increase our understanding of Disraeli the politician, his contribution to the history of the British empire, and to the emergence of a 'new' imperialism.

Disraeli was undoubtedly one of the most colourful British political characters in the nineteenth century. He was also one of the most controversial. A Christianized Jew, born into a well-established, well-to-do, middle-class family with a literary background, he was educated (until he left school at the age of fifteen) at a boarding establishment run by a Unitarian. With his 'olive complexion and coal-black eyes', and frequently bizarre appearance and behaviour, he was an exotic figure to contemporaries. His rival, the great commoner prime minister of the nineteenth century, William Gladstone ('the People's William'), was born into an extremely wealthy Liverpool merchant family with sugar plantations in the West Indies; he was educated at Eton and Christ Church, Oxford, and his father had become an MP when William was seven. Disraeli, by contrast, remained an 'outsider' for the whole of his life. Taunts of 'Shylock', 'the Jew adventurer', and 'a cursed old Jew, not worth his weight in cold bacon', delivered by opponents and colleagues alike, remained with him throughout his political career.

Nominally leader of the Conservatives in the House of Commons by 1849, his leadership of the party, even after a brief spell as prime minister in 1868, was still in question in 1872. Only with the ministry of 1874–80 did his position become more secure. Even then he presided over a seriously divided Cabinet from which two secretaries of state (the foreign and colonial secretaries) resigned in 1878 in protest at his actions. Following a much more public battle with Gladstone over the conduct of foreign policy and the future character of the empire (a quarrel which has been described as 'one of the great set-pieces of Victorian history'), Disraeli was decisively defeated at the polls in 1880. With his leadership of his party finally beyond dispute, he died, already something of a legend, in 1881.

To contemporaries, including his closest friends, Disraeli was an enigma. On the day of his death a colleague described him as 'a puzzle and a subject of wonder'. Disraeli deliberately cultivated this air of mystery. An early biographer, W. F. Monypenny, concluded that mystery was 'of the essence of the man'. And so the controversies surrounding Disraeli during his lifetime refused to die with him. Even today, historians find it impossible to reach a consensus about the man and his political career.

Disraeli's blatant careerism, his naked opportunism, his arcane political machinations, his deep love of intrigue, his sheer effrontery, his wildly extravagant claims, his mode of writing and speech that sometimes bordered on the fantastic, caused him to be called a cynic, a charlatan, a dreamer, a 'clever conjurer'. For nearly twenty-five years (except for three short interludes of minority government), he led a party that was in almost permanent opposition. Forever grasping at opportunities to unsettle ministers and unseat governments, attacking government measures without revealing his own opinions or proposing anything to the contrary, rapidly changing tack in order to discomfort opponents, forming unlikely alliances to achieve short-term ends, normally following the path most likely to keep his own party united, he developed opposition into a fine art. One of Disraeli's friends and political associates, Edward Stanley (later fifteenth earl of Derby), recorded in his diary in July 1850: 'there is certainly a very prevalent impression that Disraeli has no well-defined opinions of his own; but is content to adopt, and defend, any which may be popular with the Conservative party at the time.'

It is hardly surprising that some historians have seen him simply as a poseur, an adventurer without political principle, driven by personal dislike of Sir Robert Peel and Gladstone and a love of power and patronage, whose main achievement was the making of his own political career. Ian Machin, in the most recent commentary, maintains that in Disraeli's eyes party and his personal political fortunes were paramount. He was 'entirely pragmatic in the way he took up and discarded policies' in his quest to gain and keep political power. He was 'completely without any ideological prescriptions which might have made loyal service to ideals a more compelling demand than even rising to a powerful position'.

A number of historians have adopted a rather more favourable stance towards Disraeli. One group, dubbed appropriately enough the 'neo-opportunist school', believe that Disraeli did have principles but that — so great an opportunist was he — it is frequently impossible to reconcile his words with his deeds, his actions often being totally inconsistent. Lord Blake's assessment is that Disraeli, the practical politician *par excellence,* 'never abandoned or denied his own "philosophy" but it had little effect on his actions . . . Disraeli had learned long ago that the art of politics is the art of the possible, though he had not, perhaps, learned that lesson when he first adumbrated the "Tory idea" '. While the ideas of politicians are usually tempered by circumstances once they gain office, this still sounds very much like special pleading.

Others, however, have suggested that not only can continuity of purpose be traced throughout Disraeli's political career but that, within the broader framework of reconciling continuity and change, his principles *and* actions remained remarkably consistent. Tactics may have changed but not Disraeli's objectives. C. S. Lewis has argued that Disraeli believed that 'the primary duty of a statesman was conservation of the divinely originated heritage'. Disraeli was convinced that the

> great need of the age was a restoration of faith in those sacred ideals embodied in such traditional English institutions as the old agrarian community, the common law, the Church, and the Monarchy . . . A review of Disraeli's policy, from beginning to end, reveals a striking consistency. At all times he attempted to further causes which to his way of thinking would foster popular attachment to traditional institutions. (C. J. Lewis, 'Theory *versus* expediency in the policy of Disraeli', *Victorian Studies,* 4 (1961), 240, 258)

Paul Smith has recently re-emphasized the importance of the principles enunciated by Disraeli at the beginning of his political career. These were repeated in the general preface to a new edition of his novels in 1870. It is impossible, concludes Smith, to dismiss Disraeli's 'extensive and coherent set of observations on English history, character and destiny', reiterated so steadfastly over a period of fifty years, 'as a mere bag of burglar's tools for effecting felonious entry to the British political pantheon'. And so the argument goes on.

This division of opinion is reflected in the discussion of Disraeli's role in British imperial history. Was Disraeli a prophet and pioneer of the New Imperialism or merely a charlatan intent on short-term political gain? Controversy surrounds his attitude towards colonies, his policy towards the empire, his contribution to the character of British imperialism, and his role in the onset of the New Imperialism.

Certainly in contemporary minds Disraeli's name and 'imperialism' had become inextricably entwined by the time of the 1880 election. Sir John Seeley, in his Cambridge lectures on 'The Expansion of England' published in 1883, was in no doubt that it was Disraeli who had eclipsed the 'Little England' ideas of Gladstone and the Liberals. Indeed, as the 'Great Depression' deepened and the 'Scramble for Africa' began in earnest, many people came to regard the empire as a panacea for most of Britain's ills. With the benefit of hindsight, Disraeli's imagination and foresight began to be appreciated anew. By the time the first *Short History of British Colonial Policy* came to be written by H. E. Egerton in 1897, Disraeli's reputation for having inaugurated a new phase of British imperial expansion with his rallying cry to the party faithful at the Crystal Palace in June 1872 was firmly entrenched. This view was powerfully underscored by Disraeli's official biographer, George Buckle.

Completing Monypenny's *Life of Benjamin Disraeli* in 1920, Buckle chronicled Disraeli's life-long belief in the benefits of empire and listed the great additions of territory made during the 1874–80 ministry. He apotheosized the Crystal Palace address as 'the famous declaration from which the modern conception of the British Empire largely takes its rise'. Disraeli's affirmation that maintenance of empire was one of the three great objectives of the Conservative party was a creative and prophetic act inaugurating the party's much-vaunted association with empire. According to Buckle, this far-sighted statesman was one of the principal architects of the twentieth-century empire and of Britain's continuing greatness.

Critics of this assessment soon made their views known and a rather different interpretation began to find favour. J. L. Morison, a Scottish Gladstonian Liberal, began the attack. Reviewing Monypenny and Buckle's six-volume biography, he argued that Disraeli had shown little foresight or inspiration where the empire was concerned and completely misunderstood 'the essence of the modern British Commonwealth'. In fact, he lived in a completely unreal world, remained utterly ignorant of colonial questions, and was panic-stricken by the most ordinary difficulties of colonial administration. Disraeli's imperialism was a sham that brought discredit on Great Britain. His foreign policy had been equally unrealistic and immoral: 'by his audacious and spirited use of British credit and moral power in Europe, touched with the successful gambler's gift of trickery, he set the nation high among the predatory powers of Europe'. It was a powerful indictment.

It was a view soon endorsed by the distinguished Danish scholar,

C. A. Bodelsen, whose influential *Studies in Mid-Victorian Imperialism* (1924) helped to establish the orthodox interpretation of British imperial history that held sway until well after the Second World War. Bodelsen maintained that Disraeli's adoption of the imperial idea was due 'less to his own conviction of the greatness of the cause of Imperialism than to the realization that here was a new chance of "dishing the Whigs" and of monopolizing for the Conservatives a cause which was sure to be popular with the constituencies'. Prior to 1872, Disraeli had shown little interest in colonies except where some party advantage could be obtained, as Goldwin Smith, Grant Duff and Sir William Gregory attested. In fact, he was an outright separatist in the 1850s and 1860s, calling colonies 'a millstone round our necks' in 1852 and 'dead-weights' in 1866. Clearly, Disraeli had adopted the imperial mantle in 1872 out of sheer opportunism. Furthermore, his Crystal Palace speech contained nothing original, revealed great ignorance of colonial conditions, and the ideas put forward were totally impractical. No attempt was made to implement them after 1874.

Nevertheless, the new empire sentiment had been successfully annexed to the Conservative party. Bodelsen also conceded that Disraeli did have a share in adding two elements to British imperialism: 'jingoism', and 'the particular brand of Imperialism which Seeley called the bombastic school, i.e. the school of Imperialism which dwells on the spectacular aspect of the possession of colonies, which is prone to consider mere extent of territory an advantage in itself, and which glories in the possession of "an Empire on which the sun never sets"'.

This analysis fitted perfectly the framework of the history of the nineteenth-century empire that Bodelsen did so much to promote: an age of limited interest in empire after 1815, of anti-imperialism almost, followed by a dramatic 'turn of the tide' in the years immediately following 1870, which ushered in an age of jingoism and belligerent expansionism that lasted until the First World War. Disraeli seemed to personify these developments: initially a 'separatist', he suddenly changed his clothes to adopt his imperialist garb in 1872, mainly for party gain. Subsequently, in tune with the times, he became a sabre-rattling empire enthusiast and a confirmed expansionist during his second ministry. It was a cynical performance, typical of Disraeli's 'unprincipled' conduct in other fields. This soon became the standard interpretation of Disraeli's imperialist antics and may still be found in some textbooks today.

Forty years on, Bodelsen's views still held good. They received further endorsement, with some modification, in Richard Koebner's and Helmut D. Schmidt's semantic survey, *Imperialism: The Story and Significance of a Political Word, 1840–1960* (1964). Koebner and Schmidt agreed that Disraeli's concern for the British empire was completely new and unexpected: Disraeli was merely indulging in a piece of demagogic self-advertisement at a time when his leadership of the party was under attack. The Crystal Palace speech, in reality a criticism in retrospect of previous Liberal policy and not intended as a statement of future Conservative plans, was poorly received in the press. Its renown, therefore, was totally unjustified. In sharp contrast to Bodelsen, Koebner and Schmidt concluded that it was quite mistaken to believe that the Crystal Palace speech forged an ideological link between championship of empire and Conservatism. The authors, however, agreed with Bodelsen's assessment of Disraeli's contribution to the character of British imperialism and, in two path-breaking chapters covering Indian policy and conduct of the Eastern Question, charted in detail, for the first time, the establishment of 'imperialism' in the late 1870s as a slogan in British party strife.

The existing state of research was faithfully reflected in Robert Blake's magisterial biography of Disraeli published in 1966. Blake did not devote anywhere near as much space to a discussion of Disraeli's imperial role as the authorized biographers had done earlier in the century. Nor did he seem interested in discovering what Disraeli's 'imperialism' was really all about. It was, perhaps, a reflection of the decline of empire and contemporary disenchantment with the Commonwealth. However, in the wake of the pioneering works of Ronald Robinson and Jack Gallagher, arguing the case for continuity in British policy towards the empire in the nineteenth century, Imperial and Commonwealth studies were undergoing an historiographical revolution. In the process, the older framework of Britain's imperial history, with its neat divide about 1870, was demolished. Discussion rapidly spread to attitudes towards the colonies and revisionist historians were soon at work on Disraeli. Unfortunately, the product of their labours appeared too late to be included in Blake's biography.

In the mid-1960s, students of British imperial policy examined Disraeli's imperial ideas afresh. After perusing Disraeli's earlier statements about empire, S. R. Stembridge asserted that, far from having adopted new ideas for political gain in 1872, most of the points in Disraeli's Crystal Palace address could be found in his letters and speeches dating back to the 1830s and 1840s. Even the attempt to equate the Liberals with the separatists was not new: Disraeli had attempted to do just that in his famous jibe against 'prigs and pedants' in 1863. In fact, the whole of the Crystal Palace speech had been foreshadowed a decade earlier. Stembridge was also able to show that the much-quoted references to millstones and dead-weights were not typical of Disraeli's remarks: they were no more than momentary outbursts of irritation when Disraeli was chancellor of the Exchequer. Stembridge concluded that while it might seem plausible to dismiss Disraeli's imperialism as a mere electioneering device, it simply was not justified: 'he spoke too often of the importance of the Empire to British strength and prestige for historians to doubt his sincerity or to believe that he was simply an opportunist mouthing the popular slogans of the moment.'

Interestingly, Stembridge went on to argue that if Disraeli was not a separatist in the 1860s, neither was he an expansionist in the 1870s. He paid scant attention to colonial affairs during his ministry and showed no interest in expanding the empire. He disliked the Ashanti war as much as he objected to the Zulu war. He did not seek territory in Egypt. Only in India, where 'masterly inactivity' was thrown over, was a new imperial policy adopted. But that was to be expected since the possession of India was central to Disraeli's conception of Britain's position in the world. Disraeli's 'imperial ideal was a powerful England strengthened by the resources and peoples of a far-flung empire, playing a decisive role in world affairs'.

This reassessment was fully confirmed by the more detailed researches of W. D. McIntyre, C. F. Goodfellow and Maurice Cowling. McIntyre exploded once and for all the myth of a series of 'forward movements' in 1874 — in West Africa, the South Pacific and the Malay States — resulting from a new Conservative philosophy of empire. Inheriting a series of crises in the tropics, the Conservatives did little more than implement the policies initiated by their predecessors. In each region a policy of minimum intervention was followed. McIntyre also pointed out that Disraeli played little part in these matters. His sole contribution consisted of a few letters of encouragement (not advice) to the colonial secretary, Lord Carnarvon, aimed at flattering a difficult colleague.

The pattern was repeated in South Africa. In 1966, Goodfellow showed how Carnarvon had resurrected his predecessor's confederation scheme and, when this failed, engineered the annexation of the Transvaal. Even the Zulu war, which brought the humiliation of defeat at Isandlwana, was not the result of any aggressive or expansionist scheme. The governor of Cape Colony had defied Colonial Office instructions and presented an ultimatum to the Zulu king. While Disraeli supported the governor in public, privately he thought he should be impeached.

Maurice Cowling contended that a similar situation occurred in Afghanistan. Here, another rebellious pro-consul, ignoring instructions from home, created a situation which resulted in war and the massacre of a British military mission in Kabul. Again, Disraeli defended his viceroy in public, talking grandly of securing a 'scientific frontier'; in private, he was furious. Once more, Disraeli's weakness as prime minister, his failure to oversee departmental ministers and control local representatives, had led to totally unforeseen and unwanted complications.

In fact, the more Disraeli's record in the 1874–80 ministry was probed, the quicker his reputation as an imperialist seemed to evaporate. The purchase of the Suez Canal Company shares was not the great triumph it was made out to be. It was the Queen who had pressurized a reluctant prime minister into enacting the Royal Titles Bill. The occupation of Cyprus was entirely the work of Lord Salisbury. Slowly, the legend of Disraeli, the great champion of empire, was pulled apart. D. C. Gordon concluded that Disraeli extended nothing more than an 'histrionic embrace' to the idea of expansion: 'Disraeli's imperialism was essentially rhetorical: it added little to the empire's power.' Once again, it seemed impossible to match Disraeli's words with his deeds, and the 'neo-opportunist' school of argument received a further boost. By 1976, Disraeli's star had sunk so low that in Ronald Hyam's *Britain's Imperial Century, 1815–1914*, a tale 'without heroes', Disraeli hardly rates a mention. His much discussed contribution to the British empire seemed little more than a myth.

Such an analysis was not destined to go unchallenged. In many ways the pendulum had swung too far. True, Disraeli was not interested in the self-governing colonies, the government of indigenous peoples, or expansion in the tropics, except in so far as these problems impinged on Great Britain's foreign policy and its prestige as a world power. It was the part the possession of empire could play in assisting Great Britain's role in world affairs that had interested him most. The key to Disraeli's imperial ideas lay in the conduct of Indian business and in his handling of the Eastern Question crisis when, in speech after speech, a new vision of empire emerged: of a centralized military empire backing up the strength of Great Britain in her role as a world power, providing both resources and armies beyond the control of Parliament. It was the advertising of this concept that led to the rise of jingoism and a running battle with Gladstone, over the future character of the empire, in the gladiatorial combat of 1876–80.

In 1974, Ira Klein provided further information about Disraeli's responsibility for the Afghan War. And in two articles published in 1982 and 1989, P. J. Durrans re-examined the Liberal attack on 'Beaconsfieldism'. Disraeli's Liberal critics feared that imperialism abroad might become imperialism at home with Parliament undermined, the royal prerogative exalted, and the door opened to personal rule, thereby corrupting public life and degrading the national character. It was not so much what Disraeli did and said that frightened Gladstone and his supporters, as what Disraeli was thought capable of doing. Disraeli was accused of having a grand design aimed at subverting the moral character and liberal representative traditions of the British political system. In this way, many contemporaries came to credit Disraeli with a very consistent Machiavellian purpose.

The historiographical merry-go-round came full circle in 1980 with the publication of a provocative article by Freda Harcourt who argued that Disraeli had indeed 'set Britain on the path of the "new" imperialism'. Unlike Buckle, however, she chose 1867, rather than 1872 or 1874–80, as the key date. In a world where Great Britain's international prestige had recently suffered several blows, and at a time of great political, social, and economic upheaval, Disraeli sensed that 'a show of aggression, if free from risk, would be popular'. If it were to symbolize a renewal of past imperial splendour, it would focus the energies of the whole nation and 'provide a foundation for national unity more compelling than any other that could be devised at the time'. This new phase of imperialism was signalled by the Abyssinian expedition: 'Forceful, deliberate and chauvinistic, it was in such marked contrast to the inertia and hesitancy recently typical of attitudes to foreign and imperial affairs that it constituted a decisive break with the past.' Thus, some five years later at the Crystal Palace, Disraeli could make his appeal on behalf of the empire confident in the knowledge that he had 'already tested the reactions of the working classes to the great national impulses of war and imperialism and found the response positive'.

Was Disraeli about to be reinstated as the pioneer of the New Imperialism? Unfortunately, there is little evidence to support some of Harcourt's assertions and her central thesis was challenged by Nini Rodgers in 1984. Nevertheless, in placing imperial affairs firmly within their home and foreign policy contexts, Harcourt performed a useful service. The relationship between domestic politics and foreign policy between 1865 and 1885 was re-examined by Marvin Swartz in 1985 and the empire began to be absorbed back into the mainstream of Disraeli studies. P. R. Ghosh attempted to weave imperial affairs into his financial approach to Disraelian Conservatism in 1984 and, in 1990, J. K. Walton placed a chapter on 'Nation and Empire' at the heart of his Lancaster Pamphlet on Disraeli.

Alas, this is not to suggest that a consensus is beginning to emerge. Just as Freda Harcourt could ignore the work of Stembridge when taking 1867 as the starting-point of Disraeli's imperialism, so could Ghosh continue to argue that for Disraeli 'the mere maintenance of empire was a vast obligation and a source of material weakness . . . In private the colonies were always deadweights.' Perhaps J. L. Morison was not too far from the mark when he predicted, in 1920, that the character and value of Disraelian imperialism were likely to remain the 'storm-centre' of Disraeli's life.

We are left, then, with a series of questions to which there are no agreed answers. What was the nature of Disraeli's beliefs about empire in the years before 1867? How profoundly and how consistently were they held and for what reason? Did Disraeli inaugurate the New Imperialism by deliberately launching the Abyssinian expedition in 1867 and to what end? What was the significance of the Crystal Palace speech in 1872? Did Disraeli's return to office herald the implementation of a new Conservative philosophy of empire? To what extent was the ministry of 1874–80 an expansionist one? What part did Disraeli play in the administration of colonial affairs? What light does the conduct of the Eastern Question throw on Disraeli's imperial ideas? Why had 'imperialism' become a slogan in party strife by 1880? What contribution did Disraeli make to the history of the British empire and the development of British imperialism? What role did he play in the beginnings of the New Imperialism? The ensuing chapters survey each of these problems in turn and, in the light of recent research, identify some broad issues on which agreement may be reached.

2. The Anti-imperialist?

Any examination of imperial ideas in the years between the Reform Acts of 1832 and 1867 is bound to be bedevilled by a number of factors, especially if the object is to investigate consistency of thought and purpose. The empire of the early nineteenth century was undergoing a period of rapid change. Following the dramatic loss of the American colonies, Adam Smith's celebrated attack on the 'old colonial system' in his *Wealth of Nations*, and minor rebellions in British North America in 1837, the two main props of the eighteenth-century empire — direct control over economic policy and autocratic government from Whitehall — were slowly removed. The gradual dismantling of the ramshackle series of commercial and navigation laws known as 'mercantilism' and the introduction of responsible government — the handing over of control of internal affairs to locally elected assemblies — in most of the colonies of British settlement necessitated a complete restructuring of the imperial relationship. Contemporaries had not only to grapple with the administrative implications of the new doctrines, but to adjust their ideas and attitudes towards the costs and benefits of colonies. The empire of the early 1870s was a very different institution from that of forty years previously.

In fact, the empire was such a heterogeneous and amorphous collection of colonies, protectorates and protected states, so loose and sometimes accidental an association of units with few shared characteristics and no coherence in government, that contemporaries frequently found it difficult to take a coherent view of such diverse possessions. Consequently, views changed not only over time but with the area under discussion, and in accordance with whatever concern was foremost in the minds of individuals. In the age of free trade, some thought colonies had lost their commercial value and were simply a burden on the Exchequer. These people were called 'Little Englanders', separatists, or anti-imperialists; many were followers of Cobden and Bright whom Disraeli dubbed the 'school of Manchester'. Others welcomed the introduction of responsible government as the way most likely to remove the burdens on mother country and colony alike and thereby preserve the imperial connection — these were the Colonial Reformers. Disraeli belonged to neither group: he was a consolidationist. Although he came to realize that, as with free trade, it was not possible or necessarily desirable to turn back the clock, he regretted the hurried way in which British control had been withdrawn and persistently called for the relationship to be remodelled.

Any reconstruction of Disraeli's imperial ideas, however, faces a number of problems. The evidence is piecemeal and scattered. Gladstone served nine months' apprenticeship in the Colonial Office in 1835 and 1845, had a passionate interest in the details of colonial administration which led him to intervene regularly in colonial debates, and wrote pamphlets and other theoretical works on colonial topics. Disraeli had none of this experience. Indeed, most historians agree that he had very little interest in administrative detail; during his entire political career he held only one administrative office (that of chancellor of the Exchequer, on three occasions). 'He detests details', Carnarvon fumed. 'He does no work . . . Mr Corry [Disraeli's secretary] is in fact Prime Minister.' Even when putting policies into effect, Machin notes that Disraeli much preferred to dazzle by triumphant strokes: 'He would be at the centre of political action himself when a *coup* was being executed, but when the enactment of policy required calm, steady planning and humdrum deliberation he would sometimes (though not always) leave the practical work to others while patronising them with his support.' He was a master of ideas, not details. Disraeli's imperial ideas before 1867, therefore, often have to be gleaned from writings and speeches on such topics as finance, parliamentary reform, Indian and foreign affairs. He did take up colonial questions, but often in a partisan manner with the intention of wielding a stick to beat the government or to make a political point not always sincerely held.

Disraeli does not seem to have thought deeply about empire and colonies until 1849, when he took his place on the Tory front bench. Thereafter, he constantly sought to establish some generally agreed principles that would allow him to put forward a Conservative view of colonial policy and gain some political advantage for his party. He received little support from Lord Stanley, however, and the idea had to be discarded while Stanley (later fourteenth earl of Derby) remained official party leader. At the Crystal Palace in June 1872, Disraeli seized the opportunity to resurrect his ideas and put a long-considered strategy into operation, with the intention of rallying his party and making his own position as leader more secure.

Disraeli's earliest references to empire, though sporadic, are none the less revealing. The empire is normally seen as a prop and symbol of Britain's greatness, to the preservation of which a 'national' party should be dedicated. In his first political pamphlet, *'What is He?'* (1833), written while still only a candidate for Parliament, Disraeli wrote in his typically florid style of the current political divisions (no doubt with his own future role in mind):

> It would sometimes appear that the loss of our great Colonial Empire must be the necessary consequence of our prolonged domestic dissensions. Hope, however, lingers to the last. In the sedate but vigorous character of the British nation we may place great confidence. Let us not forget also an influence too much underrated in this age of bustling mediocrity — the influence of individual character. Great spirits may yet arise to guide the groaning helm through the world of troubled waters — spirits whose proud destiny it may still be at the same time to maintain the glory of the Empire, and to secure the happiness of the People. (William Hutcheon (ed.), *Whigs and Whiggism: Political Writings by Benjamin Disraeli* (London, John Murray, 1913), 22)

In contesting the constituency of Taunton in a by-election in 1835, and having changed allegiance from Radical to Tory, Disraeli stated:

> As the question 'What is he?' has been repeated by Mr. Bunter, I should wish to reply to it, that hereafter there may be no mistake. When I first entered into political life, I found the high places of the realm filled by the party of which my opponent is a member . . . I believed that if the Whigs remained in office for any length of time, this glorious, this unrivalled Empire would perish for ever — I considered it my duty to oppose the Whigs, and to ensure their discomfiture and, if possible, their destruction as a party. (T. E. Kebbel, *Selected Speeches of the Late Right Honourable Earl of Beaconsfield*, vol.I (London, Longmans, Green, 1882), 28)

Having failed to gain the support of the electors of Taunton, Disraeli attacked the Melbourne government in a series of scurrilous and anonymous leading articles in the *Morning Post* in August and

September 1835. Then, in 1836, under the pseudonym of 'Runnymede', he addressed a series of open letters to several leading politicians. There is some wit and much invective. The womanizing, rouged Palmerston is the 'Lord Fanny of diplomacy', and the nonchalant Melbourne is accused of 'sauntering over the destinies of a nation and lounging away the glory of an Empire'. One of his best lampoons was of the colonial secretary, Lord Glenelg, who had a reputation for indolence. He wrote satirically,

> I forget who was the wild theorist who enunciated the absurd doctrine that 'ships, colonies and commerce' were the surest foundation of the empire. What an infinitely ridiculous idea! But the march of intellect and the spirit of the age have cleansed our brains of this perilous stuff ... **[DOCUMENT I]**

In 'To the House of Lords', he wrote:

> there is not a man in Britain who at the bottom of his heart is not proud of our empire . . . The English nation formed the empire. Ours is the imperial isle. England is the Metropolitan country, and we might as well tear out the living heart from the human form, and bid the heaving corpse still survive, as suppose that a great empire can endure without some concentration of power and vitality. (Hutcheon, op. cit., 314, 315–16)

And in 'To the People':

> your flag still floats triumphant in every division of the globe, in spite of the menaces of dismemberment that threaten your empire from every quarter. Neither domestic nor foreign agitation has yet succeeded in uprooting your supremacy. But how long this imperial integrity may subsist, when it is the object of a faction in your own land to array great classes of your population in hostile collision, and when, from the Castle of Dublin to the Castle of Quebec, your honour is tampered with by the deputies of your sovereign, is a question which well deserves your quick and earnest consideration. (Ibid., 272–3)

After the 1837 rebellions in the Canadas, Disraeli asked, in the 'Old England' series of letters in *The Times*, in January 1838, how the Queen's government was to be maintained. 'The whole nation cries out: "Question, question".' **[DOCUMENT II]** He called for 'a powerful colonial system, involving the interests of the merchant, the manufacturer, and the shipowner'. In 1840, he was still toying with a union between the Conservative party and the 'Radical masses' as the only means of preserving the empire from a domestic oligarchy, intent, under the guise of Liberalism, on 'denationalizing' England. Fortunately, the 'national character may yet save the Empire'.

All this is typical of Disraeli in his early years — accusing political opponents of trying to dismantle the empire, the emphasis on the ancient institutions of the land, the need to create a national party to defend the empire and ensure 'the happiness of the people' if the country were to stay great — and it remained part of his repertoire in later years, the rhetoric becoming more extravagant and the presentation more flamboyant once he was in power. In the 1840s, Disraeli also showed great interest in the Indian empire, contributing at length to debates on the first Afghan War.

Perhaps it is not too fanciful to detect some of Disraeli's more flamboyant ideas concerning India in a passage from his novel *Tancred*, published in 1847, in which Fakredeen, an emir of the Lebanon, suggests one way of bringing back empire to the East:

> You must . . . quit a petty and exhausted position for a vast and prolific empire. Let the Queen of the English collect a great fleet, let her stow away all her treasure, bullion, gold plate, and precious arms; be accompanied by all her court and chief people, and transfer the seat of her empire from London to Delhi. There she will find an immense empire ready made, a first rate army, and a large revenue . . . We will acknowledge the Empress of India as our suzerain, and secure for her the Levantine coast. If she like, she shall have Alexandria as she now has Malta: it could be arranged. (*Tancred* 1847, 263)

And so it very nearly was. Partly as a result of Disraeli's later actions, by 1911 Great Britain did control Alexandria and a King-Emperor had held court in Delhi, the centre of Britain's eastern empire.

Of more immediate concern were the effects of the victory of free-trade ideas on the imperial relationship. Disraeli lamented 'the destruction of our colonial system', expressing the belief that 'we should ere long have to reconstruct it'. Speaking at Newport Pagnell in 1847, however, he made it clear that the protection he advocated for the country was of a moderate, imperial character:

> They had heard much of the Customs Union of Germany, but when they looked to the numerous colonies over which the Queen of this country ruled, they saw Great Britain possessing a greater area than any other European Power, except Russia, and they were tempted to ask why should not England have her Imperial Union, the produce of

every clime coming in free which acknowledged her authority, and paying no tax to the public Exchequer? (W. F. Monypenny and G. E. Buckle, *The Life of Benjamin Disraeli, Earl of Beaconsfield*, vol.III (London, John Murray, 1914), 25)

It was an idea — one of many — to which Disraeli constantly returned during the next two decades.

In 1849, widening his campaign against the 'economic phantasies of the hour' to include Earl Grey's introduction of internal self-government into Canada, Nova Scotia and New Brunswick, Disraeli urged the Commons not to sacrifice 'the surest sources of your wealth and the most certain support of your power'. He was even prepared to contemplate an alliance with the Colonial Reformers in order to bring the Russell government down. He refused Sir Charles Adderley's offer to join the council of a new 'Society for the Reform of Colonial Government', but urged Lord Stanley to capitalize on the fact that the Colonial Reformers were determined to be troublesome. It was important to decide upon the course to be taken by the party: 'I am now pretty well qualified to listen to your ideas and instructions on this head . . . as I have given a good deal of time during the recess to the Colonial question in all its branches.' When Stanley counselled against collaboration, Disraeli hoped, on 28 December 1849, that it might still be possible for the party to support a motion which would allow either himself or someone else to

> completely develop our own Colonial system, and express our own tenets on all the great points of local government, emigration, waste lands, penal settlements, etc. . . . In this Colonial discussion we must deal with frankness with the commercial question. Can we again establish a commercial tie with the Colonies without the odium of inflicting high prices on the metropolitan consumer? Could this be done by terminating all import duties whatever on Colonial produce? By really making them integral portions of the United Kingdom? No sugar duties on either Indies, and a duty on foreign corn, might set the more important colonies on their legs (a duty on foreign timber still existing), and would comprise some elements of popularity.
>
> I conclude it is too late to introduce thirty Colonial MPs into St Stephen's. Were it possible it would be a great element of future strength to the Conservative party of this country. (Ibid., 236–7)

Although Lord Stanley showed no interest, Disraeli used a debate on the repeal of the malt tax in July 1850 to call for the consolidation of 'this still, I hope, great empire', the basis of Britain's political power and commercial wealth.

Encouraged by Edward Stanley (Lord Stanley's son), Disraeli again bombarded his chief with proposals concerning colonial representation in December 1851, this time linking it with a proposed government reform bill. Disraeli suggested that the appointment of colonial MPs to vacancies occasioned by corrupt disfranchized boroughs would prevent 'the increase of the town or democratic power, without the odium of directly resisting its demands'. Lord Stanley (now earl of Derby) responded with a detailed description of the problems of colonial representation. Not to be outdone, Disraeli reminded him of the successful operation of the American North-West Ordinance in bringing the representatives of new states into Congress on an equal footing with those from the original thirteen. A similar move would 'tranquillise the Colonies, revive their affection to the Metropolis, and widen the basis and sympathies of our party'.

In the face of Derby's refusal to move, Disraeli was reduced to protesting, in the House of Commons in February 1852, at the dismantling of the colonial system in 'deference to the dogmas of political economists and of abstract enquirers'. Imperial consolidation, he argued, was now urgent. Addressing his constituents, he warned that 'whether our colonial empire shall be maintained and confirmed' was one of the great issues facing the country.

Given Disraeli's commitment to imperial consolidation, it is surprising that the short-lived Conservative ministry of February–December 1852 continued the policy of handing over control of unoccupied land to the Australian colonists (something already conceded to Canadians). But the government was in a minority, the ministers were inexperienced and Disraeli was preoccupied with his budget. He did take an interest in the second Burmese war — 'a subject on which I have long and deeply reflected'. Remember Afghanistan in 1839–41, he urged. Some had claimed the Hindu Kush was India's natural boundary: 'what a rash and ignorant dogma! And what disasters followed its adoption!' He reminded Derby:

> The Indian revenue has already a deficit of one million and a half sterling. A prolonged war must increase it. We cannot distinguish Indian from English finance ultimately; we cannot permit the Indian Government to be bankrupt. I need not point out the inevitable consequences on our Exchequer. (Ibid., 397–8)

In the end, only Lower Burma was annexed.

Soon in opposition again, Disraeli became embroiled even more closely in Indian affairs. Having sat on select committees of the House of Commons investigating the government of both India and Ceylon, he was convinced that the system of government introduced in 1833 (in which control was divided between the East India Company, with its governor-general in India, and a British government Board of Control with a cabinet minister at its head) ought to be replaced with the direct assumption of authority by Crown and Parliament. Although Disraeli lost his initial battle — the majority of his party was unwilling to unite with men such as Bright — within five years it fell to Disraeli, as leader of the House in 1858, to oversee the final transfer of the government of India to the Crown with the establishment of the British *raj*.

The outbreak of the Indian Mutiny in May 1857 confirmed Disraeli's worst suspicions of government policy. He had long been critical of the Whig policy of 'civilizing' (i.e. Westernizing) India begun by Lord William Bentinck (governor-general, 1828–35) and recently pushed forward by Lord Dalhousie (1848–56). In particular, he opposed the doctrine of 'lapse' and the annexation of Oudh. As an amateur orientalist, whose imagination had been fired by a tour in the Levant in 1830–1, he believed that Indian traditions and customs should be respected. In a speech in Parliament on 27 July 1857, notable for its calm assessment of the situation, Disraeli took issue with the view that the rising was a mere protest at the violation of a taboo: 'The rise and fall of empires are not affairs of greased cartridges.' Recent policy had disaffected every class and every caste. In future, relations between the Indian people and 'their real Ruler and Sovereign, Queen Victoria' should be drawn tighter and a guarantee given that the Queen would respect their laws, customs and religion. He thus set out the basis for the royal proclamation in 1858 and anticipated his policy of the mid-1870s. In discounting many of the atrocity stories, he also foreshadowed his later dismissal of similar events in Bulgaria in 1876. He denounced the popular demand for reprisals: 'I for one protest against taking Nana Sahib as a model for the conduct of the British soldier. I protest at meeting atrocities by atrocities.' **[DOCUMENT III]**

All in all, it was a remarkable performance. In fact, much of Disraeli's second spell in office, in the minority government of February to June 1858, was taken up with passing the new Government of India Bill ending the rule of the East India Company. Back on the opposition benches five months later, however, Disraeli's mind returned to the anomalies left by the grant of responsible government, especially the problem of military defence. He was acutely conscious of the increasing power of the United States, the growth of China and the Westernization of Japan. He reminded his constituents in a speech at Aylesbury in 1859:

> The day is coming . . . when the question of the balance of power cannot be confined to Europe alone . . . Remember always that England, though she is bound to Europe by tradition, by affection, by great similarity of habits . . . is not a mere Power of the Old World. Her geographical position, her laws, her language and religion, connect her as much with the New World as the Old . . . those great States which our own planting and colonising energies have created, by ties and interests which will sustain our power and enable us to play as great a part in the times yet to come as we do in these days, and as we have done in the past. (Ibid., vol.IV (1916), 231)

Disraeli's immediate concern was that Great Britain could not hope to defend Canada against American attack, yet because no military code had been agreed when responsible government was granted, Britain still had costly military obligations. When, in the early stages of the Civil War, the Palmerston government chose to send British troops to Canada, Disraeli intervened in a speech that earned the praise of the Colonial Reformers, to warn against dampening the ardour of the Canadians for their own defence. And Disraeli was as shocked as they when the Canadian Parliament refused to pass a militia bill to ensure adequate local defence measures. It was an act that infuriated separatists like Goldwin Smith. In a House of Commons debate on 25 July 1862, J. A. Roebuck and the secretary of state for war, Sir George Cornewall Lewis, felt no apprehension at the possibility of a future separation. Disraeli, however, remained 'anxious to maintain our colonial empire'. He regretted the hasty grant of responsible government without 'reasonable measures of self-defence'. The remaining British obligations could endanger the empire if the mother country came to feel the burden was too great. **[DOCUMENT IV]**

Disraeli continued his attack on the views of the separatists in February 1863, with his famous jibe against 'prigs and pedants', during an allusion to the proposed cession of the Ionian Islands, a protected state since the peace of 1815. With Corfu in mind, he stated:

Within the last twenty-five years the route to our Indian possessions has been changed; and, whatever the intention of the treaties of 1815, the country has been constantly congratulated on having a chain of Mediterranean garrisons, which secured our Indian Empire. I am perfectly aware that there is a school of politicians — I do not believe they are rising politicians — who are hostile to the very principle of a British Empire. But I have yet to learn that Her Majesty's Ministers have adopted the wild opinions which have been prevalent of late. Professors and rhetoricians find a system for every contingency and a principle for every chance; but you are not going, I hope, to leave the destinies of the British Empire to prigs and pedants. The statesmen who construct, and the warriors who achieve, are only influenced by the instinct of power, and animated by the love of country. Those are the feelings and those the methods which form empires . . . there can be no question either in or out of this House that the best mode of preserving wealth is power. A country, and especially a maritime country, must get possession of the strong places of the world if it wishes to contribute to its power. (3 *Hansard* 169: 95–6)

Although the Ionian Islands were ceded to Greece, Disraeli had formulated a close connection between the British empire, power in the Mediterranean, and the defence of India.

It was no doubt amusing to hear the name of the arch-apostle of Little Englandism linked with that of Palmerston. But Disraeli had a serious purpose in attempting a distinction between the parties. In June 1863 he claimed that a pledge to maintain 'the majesty of the Empire' would be a popular and 'truly irresistible' part of a Conservative programme: 'The Liberals are of the opinion that the relations between the metropolis and the people of the colonies should be abrogated. We are not.' (*The Times*, 29 June 1863)

Disraeli repeated the Conservative commitment to the colonies in a debate on Canada on 13 March 1865: it would be a grievous political error to 'renounce, relinquish, or avoid the responsibility of upholding and maintaining their interests'. He looked forward to 'that mature hour . . . when we may lose perhaps our dependencies but gain permanent allies'. The empire was a great source of strength to Great Britain in a rapidly changing world. In such circumstances, it would be 'fatal and disastrous . . . to shrink from the duty which Providence has assigned us to fulfil'. (3 *Hansard* 177: 1575–8)o

At last, Disraeli was in a position to put his ideas into practice. With the defeat of the Gladstone Reform Bill, Derby formed a third minority Conservative government. Disraeli returned to the Exchequer and within nineteen months had finally climbed the greasy pole. In his re-election speech at Beaconsfield, a fortnight after Sadowa, Disraeli reminded his audience:

> England has outgrown the continent of Europe. The abstention of England from any unnecessary interference in the affairs of Europe is the consequence, not of her decline of power, but of her increased strength. England is no longer a mere European Power; she is the metropolis of a great maritime empire, extending to the boundaries of the farthest ocean . . . She interferes in Asia, because she is really more an Asiatic Power than a European. She interferes in Australia, in Africa, and New Zealand, where she carries on war often on a great scale . . . she has a greater sphere of action than any European Power, and she has duties devolving on her on a much larger scale. (*The Times,* 14 July 1866)

The following year, it has been claimed, Disraeli 'set Britain on the path of the "new" imperialism'.

For thirty years, Disraeli had shown a personal allegiance to the name of empire. In election addresses, pamphlets, letters and speeches, he talked incessantly of defending 'the glory of this country as a great empire'. Empire was both cause and symbol of Britain's greatness. Despite accepting the coming of free trade and the introduction of responsible government in the colonies, and playing a leading part in persuading his colleagues to accept them, Disraeli none the less viewed these developments with misgiving. He regretted that the destruction of the 'old colonial system' had been accomplished so hastily and had not been accompanied by any attempt to define colonial and imperial obligations or reconstruct the imperial relationship.

As a result, he advocated a number of ideas, concentrating in particular on the creation of a colonial *zollverein* and integrating the colonies in the United Kingdom by means of colonial representation in an imperial parliament (an idea he raised again in 1866). He wanted to make the consolidation of the empire a great Conservative principle. He did not succeed, however, in finding a plausible means of achieving this end or in attracting the support of the party leader. He remained convinced, nevertheless, that the empire had a major role to play in maintaining Britain's status as a world power. It seems perverse, therefore, that for over fifty years (and still occasionally today), Disraeli has been accused of being a separatist and an anti-imperialist.

The evidence for such accusations rests on two famous, but extremely slight, quotations unearthed by Gladstone's biographer, John Morley, and repeated by Disraeli's critics ever since. In 1852 Disraeli had informed the foreign secretary, the earl of Malmesbury, that 'these wretched Colonies will all be independent, too, in a few years and are a millstone round our necks'; **[DOCUMENT V]** and in 1866 he enquired of the prime minister, Lord Derby:

> what is the use of these colonial deadweights *which we do not govern?* . . . Leave the Canadians to defend themselves; recall the African squadron; give up the settlements on the west coast of Africa; and we shall make a saving which will, at the same time, enable us to build ships and have a good Budget. **[DOCUMENT VI]**

These few sentences have damned Disraeli in the eyes of his critics, turning him into a 'Little Englander' and a separatist, and confirming the picture of an unprincipled opportunist who hastily donned imperialist clothes in 1872 in order to seize an opportunity to 'dish the Whigs'.

It is noticeable, however, that both outbursts occurred when Disraeli was chancellor of the Exchequer, at times when budgetary difficulties were foremost in his mind. Both concerned the British North American colonies and relations with the United States which could have involved Britain in an unwelcome and costly war. The first outburst, in 1852, concerned the perennial problem of American fishermen encroaching on Canadian and Newfoundland fishing grounds. The secretary of state for war and the colonies, Pakington, had unwisely delivered an ill-timed protest during the run-up to the American presidential election which, to Disraeli's horror, caused Daniel Webster, the American secretary of state, to use inflammatory language. (An agreement was reached later with the out-going President Fillmore, as Disraeli suggested.)

The second outburst in 1866 occurred at an even more difficult time economically — a time of banking house collapses, bad harvests, alleged naval maladministration and political upheaval at home. On this occasion, the Canadians, who had failed to take full responsibility for their own defence, faced internal unrest, Fenian raids from across the border, and the possibility of a full-scale American invasion as the victorious Union army sought revenge for hostile British comment and actions during the Civil War. In opposition, Disraeli consistently called for a policy of strict neutrality, avoiding irritation and friction with Canada's southern neighbour. He also consistently protested at the failure to make proper agreements concerning colonial defence. Events he had long foreseen were about to become costly reality and interfere with his budget plans. Disraeli's irritation is perfectly understandable.

In the circumstances, Britain had to rush reinforcements to Canada. But, maintained Disraeli, the British troops should be withdrawn as soon as the war scare subsided and the Canadians, over whose policy Britain had no control, should be obliged to take full responsibility for their own defence, thus removing a costly obligation from the shoulders of the British taxpayer. It was also the line advocated by the *pro-empire* Colonial Reformers. In addition, the West African naval squadron, now largely redundant, should be withdrawn. (An all-party select committee, the year previously, had recommended withdrawing from the West African settlements with the possible exception of Sierra Leone.) This would make sufficient savings to provide a surplus for shipbuilding at a time when the rising power of the United States and the emerging dominance of Prussia in Europe made defence of the British Isles a prime necessity. This was the gist of Disraeli's remarks; they were nothing more than expressions of extreme annoyance and disclose nothing worse than a wish to redefine, not terminate, the imperial relationship. To interpret them as signalling a general aversion to empire is a gross misconception.

Given Disraeli's acute awareness of the changing international scene, his repeated emphasis on the role of the empire in securing Britain's continued greatness, his constant efforts to find ways of reconstructing the imperial relationship, and his repeated urging that the Conservative party should adopt the maintenance of the empire as one of its major planks, the Crystal Palace speech and many of Disraeli's later activities in office seem to fit into a much more coherent pattern than many historians have hitherto accepted. Perhaps Disraeli was a prophet of the New Imperialism after all.

3. The Pioneer of the New Imperialism?

In 1876, the word 'imperialism', recently used to criticize the regime of Napoleon III (which was accused of practising despotic rule at home, engaging in ostentatious military display, and embarking on aggressive policies overseas), was for the first time applied to British domestic politics. On 17 March, during the acrimonious debates on the Royal Titles Bill creating the Queen 'Empress of India', *The Times* stigmatized the new title as 'threatening the Crown with the degradation of a tawdry Imperialism'. Two weeks later, on 1 April 1876, an article in the *Fortnightly Review* referred to the 'phrases of imperialism'. The *Spectator* also took up the cry on 8 April with an item headed 'English Imperialism', and *Punch* subsequently joined in with 'Imperialism triumphant' (22 April) and 'Disraeli's newly acquired Imperialism' (6 May). During the next couple of years, as the Eastern Question crisis reached its peak, the word was gradually adopted by the Liberal opposition as a slogan condemning Disraeli's foreign and imperial policies. After Gladstone, who had retired from the Liberal leadership in 1875, inveighed against 'the party, who at home as well as abroad are striving to cajole or drive us into Imperialism', Robert Lowe, an old enemy of Disraeli, led a chorus of criticism denouncing the 'vulgar mask of Imperialism'. By the general election of 1880, Disraeli's reputation as an exponent of imperialism was firmly established, a reputation that soared to new heights as a subsequent generation watched the European powers, the United States and Japan engage in a struggle for territory and economic concessions in Africa, central and south-east Asia, the Pacific, the Far East and, finally, the Middle East in the 'Age of the New Imperialism'.

Most commentators and historians, friend and foe alike, with the benefit of hindsight have traced this development in Disraeli's political reputation to his Crystal Palace speech in June 1872, hailed by Buckle as 'the famous declaration from which the modern conception of the British empire largely takes its rise'. Even critics like Bodelsen, who questioned Disraeli's sincerity and pointed to his opportunism, admitted that the speech initiated the connection between imperialism and the Conservative party. It was Freda Harcourt who first pointed to the significance of the Derby–Disraeli ministry of 1866–8. It was during these years, she argued, that Disraeli first brought about a new orientation in imperial and foreign affairs. By launching the Abyssinian expedition, Disraeli set Britain on the path of the New Imperialism in 1867.

The years 1867–74, then, are controversial years in the development of Disraeli's imperial ideas. Besides witnessing the Abyssinian war, they saw the outcry over the colonial policy of Earl Granville (Gladstone's colonial secretary, 1868–70) which R. L. Schuyler dubbed 'the climax of anti-imperialism', Disraeli's speeches at the Manchester Free Trade Hall and the Crystal Palace, and his attempt to beat the patriotic drum in the election of 1874 — the election which produced the first Conservative majority in the House of Commons since 1846. They are years worthy of close attention.

The Abyssinian war was the first of Queen Victoria's 'little wars' to become a newspaper event. The British army was accompanied by 'special correspondents' (including H. M. Stanley and G. A. Henty), 'special artists', and an official photographic unit attached to the Royal Engineers. The progress of the expedition, in its dramatic surroundings, was followed with bated breath by the British government and with noisy acclaim by the British public through newspapers and illustrated journals. Yet it is largely a forgotten war today. It is rarely discussed by students of imperial and foreign policy and it has been even more neglected in studies of Disraeli.

Freda Harcourt, however, sees the significance of the war in a much broader context. Placing the war firmly in its domestic and international settings, her argument runs along the following lines. The years 1866–7 were years of political upheaval, economic hardship and social unrest: 'Reform, public order, economic recession, integration of the classes, concern about defence, and the challenge to Britain's international standing, were all components of the same crisis.' The economic repercussions of the financial collapse of 1866 badly affected sections of the middle classes as well as the working classes, especially the very poor and the casually employed. Unemployment, high food prices, a severe winter, a cholera epidemic, and the breakdown of the relief system created dangerous conditions for the maintenance of law and order. With the prospect of violence and looting by the 'submerged and dangerous masses', the government handled the demonstrations in Hyde Park with great delicacy and quickly passed a reform measure designed to draw the respectable working classes (as opposed to the 'yeasty scum') into the existing political system, thus legitimizing the agitation and hoping to avoid the chances of a violent eruption by the mob. It was necessary to cement the process by devising a national policy that would unite the classes behind the existing leadership: war might bind the classes in a common patriotic purpose, relieve domestic tensions by turning them outwards, and give the ruling classes a chance to act out their historic role as leaders. War might also attract new voters from the working classes to the Conservative fold. To achieve these purposes, the 'Abyssinian difficulty' lay to hand.

Disraeli seized on the idea of enhancing Britain's imperial status as the only way to reassert Britain's position as a great power in a rapidly changing world. Britain had suffered blows to her prestige over the Polish and Schleswig-Holstein questions; America had recently emerged from the throes of civil war as a growing military and economic power; and Russia had taken huge steps forward in central Asia (France similarly in Cochin China); the Suez Canal was nearing completion; and after Sadowa Prussia dominated the Continent. What better way to restore British prestige and her renown as a military power than by fighting a modern war on 'a conspicuous site where British imperial strength could be adequately but safely paraded' in the service of high moral causes? Abyssinia seemed to fulfil these requirements.

Relations with King Theodore had deteriorated after the British refused to receive an embassy which the king wished to send to Queen Victoria in 1861. The dispute smouldered until December 1863 when the British consul, ordered home by his government, was put in fetters, along with several missionaries, by the Abyssinian king. In 1866 a similar fate befell three officers sent to negotiate the consul's release, all the captives being transferred to the mountain stronghold of Magdala. Disraeli saw the chance to follow an assertive foreign policy. According to Harcourt, 'since Stanley had no previous knowledge of international affairs, Disraeli was able to influence him in this direction, a change which won general approval'. A highly publicized and costly (£9,000,000) campaign to release the twelve captives ensued. The enemy forces were shot down, the captives released, and King Theodore committed suicide. British honour was vindicated, her international reputation enhanced, and national unity restored. Conservative support also increased among urban working-class voters in London and the Home Counties. The Abyssinian war was a triumph for Disraeli, seemingly endorsing his view that the Tory party was the national party and the working classes its natural allies. In short, the Abyssinian expedition was the first essay in the new popular imperialism.

It is a fascinating and persuasive argument which has been almost universally well received, linking as it does the actions of Disraeli's first ministry with those of his second. J. K. Walton, for example, concludes that the expedition 'was a distraction from domestic discontents' which 'put down a marker in international politics to Disraeli's intentions for the future: for Harcourt shows that this was essentially *his* policy'.

But *has* she really shown this? While Harcourt's article is rich in quotations from newspapers and periodicals (giving 'a panoramic view of preoccupations as they appeared at the time'), there are very few quotations from Disraeli's private papers or published speeches, and those cited do not relate to the Abyssinian expedition. In fact, there is no examination whatsoever of the origins of the war and no evidence concerning Disraeli's role in its beginnings. Even Harcourt has to admit: 'It cannot be established that he planned it in precisely these terms, if at all.' Her case is really no more than a hypothesis. And parts of that hypothesis are by no means convincing: the repeated assumption that Abyssinia was a place where military strength could be paraded safely, that Disraeli's imperial ideas should be dated from 1866 not 1872, and that 1867 constitutes a 'turning-point' in British imperial history.

Perhaps the most damaging criticisms of Harcourt's thesis are to be found in a detailed analysis of the origins of the Abyssinian expedition itself. Nini Rodgers in 'The Abyssinian expedition of 1867–1868: Disraeli's imperialism or James Murray's war?' (*Historical Journal*, 1984) asserts that the Second Reform Act and the resort to force against King Theodore were coincidental rather than consequential and that the decision to launch a campaign was not the result of any initiative by Disraeli's Cabinet. It was the crisis in Abyssinia that provoked a crisis in Whitehall. King Theodore dictated the pace. The crisis was handled by the Foreign Office, principally by the assistant under-secretary and head of the consular department, James Murray, not by the Cabinet. The prospect of a campaign was extremely embarrassing to both the previous and the present foreign secretaries. Lord Stanley was particularly nervous. Parliament had to be recalled and rapidly escalating expenditure authorized.

Far from the government warmly embracing the idea of a campaign, it viewed it as an extremely dangerous enterprise. Success was not guaranteed. Not only was the landing of a British force on the west bank of the Red Sea a hazardous business, but the hot and arid coastal plain had to be crossed without the benefit of roads; artillery had to be manœuvred to the mountainous stronghold of the Abyssinian king; and, even then, there was no obvious strategic point to capture in order to induce his surrender. What if the Abyssinian army retreated into the mountains and refused to fight? And what chance was there of retrieving the captives alive? Would they not inevitably be murdered at the approach of the British force? Launching the invasion was clearly not an easy decision for the government to take and failure could easily have led to the downfall of a shaky administration. Once he became responsible for the campaign, the secretary of state for India, Sir Stafford Northcote, confessed to the House of Commons: 'From the moment I undertook this task, I have never known what it is to be free from anxiety.'

When, against very long odds, the expedition achieved its objectives, Lord Stanley confided to his diary: 'Thus ends more fortunately than could be expected, a war on which we embarked with extreme reluctance and only from the sense of the impossibility of doing otherwise.' Rodgers concludes, after surveying the Derby papers and other ministerial correspondence, that Disraeli, no doubt preoccupied with the Reform Bill and his budgetary plans, did not exert any influence over the foreign secretary, or the direction of events, or play a larger part than his roles as leader of the House of Commons and chancellor of the Exchequer required. This view endorses Lord Blake's conclusion that the ministry should not be seen in terms of Disraelian initiatives.

Harcourt's hypothesis remains unproven. If the Abyssinian expedition was the first step on the road to the New Imperialism, it was also a very different imperialism from that of later decades. There was no question of expanding the empire: Napier was ordered to withdraw after defeating the enemy, regardless of the political situation he left behind, and only one member of the Cabinet, the earl of Carnarvon, seems tentatively to have raised the matter of annexation and without success. True, Disraeli talked grandly of 'the elephants of Asia, bearing the Artillery of Europe, over African passes which might have startled the trapper and appalled the hunter of the Alps' and of the standard of St George being raised on the 'mountains of Rasselas', but he justified the expedition before the House of Commons in terms very different from those used in the late 1870s:

> When it was first announced that England was about to embark on a most costly and perilous expedition, merely to vindicate the honour of our Sovereign and to rescue from an unjust but remote captivity a few of our fellow-subjects, the announcement was received in more than one country with something like mocking incredulity. But we have asserted the purity of our purpose. In an age accused, and perhaps not unjustly, of selfishness, and a too great regard for material interests, it is something, in so striking and significant a manner, for a great nation to have vindicated the higher principles of humanity. It is a privilege to belong to a country which has done such deeds. (Kebbel, op. cit., vol.II, 132)

Harcourt is right, however, in pointing to the changing atmosphere of the time. Interest in empire, in the press and elsewhere, was rising as the foundation of a Colonial Society (forerunner of the present Royal Commonwealth Society), campaigns for emigration, and the subsequent outcry over Granville's colonial policy indicate. In part, this was the result of further threatening developments in the field of foreign affairs, culminating in the Franco-Prussian war, which made Britain seem increasingly vulnerable. Nobody was more aware of this than Disraeli. He stated in the Commons:

> This war represents the German revolution, a greater political event than the French revolution of the last century . . . Not a single principle in the management of our foreign affairs, accepted by all statesmen for guidance up to six months ago, any longer exists. There has not been a diplomatic tradition which has not been swept away. You have a new world, new influences at work, new and unknown objects and dangers with which to cope, at present involved in that obscurity incident to novelty in such affairs . . . The balance of power has been entirely destroyed, and the country which suffers most, and feels the effects of this great change most, is England. (Monypenny and Buckle, op. cit., vol.V (1920), 133–4)

Disraeli went on to attack the government's sorry performance in handling Russia's unilateral abrogation of the Black Sea clauses of the Treaty of Paris, 1856.

Yet following the handsome Liberal election victory in November 1868, Disraeli's general policy was one of 'utmost reserve and quietness'. Fractious opposition to a government with a majority of 110 seats was pointless and undignified; it was far better, given the nature of that government, to give it plenty of rope to hang itself. It was then partly deliberate intent, as well as the ill health which caused his absence on a number of occasions in the sessions of 1869–71, that led Disraeli to adopt a much lower profile than hitherto. Disraeli also returned to his literary activities (*Lothair* was published in 1870) and his wife was already showing signs of the cancer from which she died in late 1872. He played little part in the attack on Granville's colonial policy during 1869–70.

The new colonial secretary was thought to be an adherent of the 'Manchester School' and so from the very first his conduct of colonial affairs was kept under the microscope. Cardwell's proposed army reforms, intended to improve service conditions, the quality of officers and recruits, and to remove the unpopular service overseas, involved the withdrawal of colonial garrisons and the concentration of a smaller force in Great Britain to ensure adequate defence of the mother country. The withdrawal of the garrisons was no new policy, nor was it a party policy. One of Granville's first acts was to endorse the decision of the previous Conservative colonial secretary, the duke of Buckingham, to withdraw the last remaining British regiment from New Zealand. The same policy was also applied to Canada. Disraeli, having complained of 'bloated armaments' in 1866, was no doubt in sympathy with the government's intentions and, along with the Colonial Reformers, had advocated troop withdrawals from Canada in 1865. Granville, however, abetted by an unfortunate speech by the Canadian governor-general and some allegedly harshly worded dispatches to New Zealand, ran into a storm of protest in and out of Parliament, mainly orchestrated by Liberal backbenchers. Apart from accusing the government of wishing to establish a standing army, Disraeli refused to give a lead. Approving government actions in reducing the army presence and the accompanying cost for the British taxpayer, and never having been interested in the internal affairs of self-governing colonies, he was content to watch the Liberals tearing themselves apart. Only the earl of Carnarvon in the Lords, and the Conservative *Standard* among the press, tried to make political capital out of the controversy.

Disraeli's aloofness met with a great deal of criticism from his supporters. Given the personal animus that existed in the party against him (Salisbury and Disraeli were still not on speaking terms), and the fact that the government appeared to be under serious strain as sectional interests became alienated from the leadership, Disraeli's inactivity was no longer acceptable to many. An influential group of prominent Conservatives met secretly to discuss appointing a new leader. Realizing that trouble was afoot, Disraeli rose to the occasion, taking up the challenge of those who alleged that the Conservatives had no programme. With the intention of reasserting his leadership and rallying his party, he made two set-piece speeches to groups of constituency associations which the party organization under John Eldon Gorst had been quietly building up.

The first took place on 3 April 1872 in Lancashire where, after reviewing a parade of Conservative associations, Disraeli spoke for three and a quarter hours in Manchester's Free Trade Hall, Cobden's favourite platform during the Corn Laws crisis. 'The programme of the Conservative party is to maintain the Constitution of the country,' he announced. He went on to outline how radical forces in the government were threatening the throne, the House of Lords, the Church, the union with Ireland, and national honour and security. After a celebrated reference to the Cabinet as 'a range of exhausted volcanoes', he turned to attack the conduct of foreign policy. Concluding on a high note, he maintained that there never was a time when England's power was so great and her resources so inexhaustible:

> And yet, gentlemen, it is not merely our fleets and armies, our powerful artillery, our accumulated capital, and our unlimited credit on which I so much depend, as upon that unbroken spirit of her people, which I believe was never prouder of the Imperial country to which they belong. Gentlemen, it is to that spirit that I above all things trust . . . Proud of your confidence and encouraged by your sympathy, I now deliver to you, as my last words, the cause of the Tory Party, the English Constitution, and of the British Empire. (Kebbel, op.cit., vol.II, 522)

The second occasion was an address to the parent body of the local Conservative and Constitutional associations, the National Union, at the Crystal Palace on 24 June 1872. Here, Disraeli laid down the three great objectives of the Tory party: to maintain the institutions of the country, to uphold the empire, and to elevate the condition of the people. All three themes were matters that he had ruminated about for forty years. He reiterated his idea that the Liberals were the 'cosmopolitan' or 'continental' party and the Conservatives the 'national' party, developing the themes of patriotism, empire and the need for social reform. The working classes were the party's natural allies: the Conservatives would work to improve public health and working and living conditions. Far from being 'a policy of sewage', as some Liberals scoffed, it was a matter of life and death, of housing, health, 'air, light and water'. The working classes were proud of belonging to a great country and wished to maintain its greatness:

> The issue is not a mean one. It is whether you will be content to be a comfortable England, modelled and moulded upon Continental principles and meeting in due course an inevitable fate, or whether you will be a great country, — an Imperial country, — a country where your sons, when they rise, rise to paramount positions, and obtain not merely the esteem of their countrymen, but command the respect of the world. (Kebbel, op. cit., vol.II, 534)

Disraeli knew he could rely on 'the sublime instincts of an ancient people'.

The empire section of the speech was extremely brief. **[DOCUMENT VII]** It need not detain us here. It contained nothing new. As in 1863, Disraeli accused the Liberals of being a party of separatists, labouring to disband an empire which they regarded as a costly burden to be shed as soon as possible. As a result, self-government had not been accompanied by measures to reconstruct the relationship. Disraeli regretted that no arrangements had been made for an imperial tariff, a military code delineating home and colonial responsibilities, a guarantee that unsettled colonial lands would be available for British emigrants, or the representation of colonial views in the metropolis. This was too late now, but the colonies might yet become a source of 'incalculable strength and happiness'. No future minister would do his duty if he neglected any opportunity to reconstruct the British empire.

It was all good party propaganda, accusing the Liberals of 'money-grubbing Little Englandism'. As Koebner and Schmidt pointed out, it was a criticism in retrospect of Liberal policy, not a statement of future Conservative plans. It caused little comment in the media, the majority of newspapers ignoring the brief section on empire. Thus most of the criticisms of contemporaries and subsequent historians were unfounded or simply irrelevant. True, Disraeli chose an opportune moment to dress up some of his old ideas for personal and party gain, but this does not make him insincere. He did not pick up ideas from the pages of *Blackwood's Magazine* or suddenly change his views for propaganda purposes. The attack on Granville's policy had already subsided. The significance attached to the speech by subsequent historians as holding an important place in the history of the empire, in the annals of the Conservative party and in the development of Disraeli's imperial ideas was largely mistaken. Nevertheless, the Free Trade Hall and Crystal Palace speeches served their purpose. The sparkle of Disraeli's oratory rallied his party, restored its morale and confirmed Disraeli's leadership. The standard of a new progressive Conservatism had been raised.

By March 1873, Disraeli was scenting electoral victory. The Liberal government was disintegrating and he was determined not to form another minority government. Gladstone was obliged to soldier on until he finally called a general election in January 1874. In the hurriedly drawn up election manifesto, Disraeli accused the government of 'incessant and harassing legislation'; it would have been far better had 'there been a little more energy in our foreign policy, and a little less in our domestic legislation'. He found little in the government's colonial policy to criticize. The outcome of the Ashanti war, which Disraeli had called an unprofitable and inglorious quarrel, was still awaited. After wasting much ink accusing the government of having made an injudicious bargain with the Dutch over the Gold Coast and Sumatra, thereby incurring Ashanti hostility and losing control over the Straits of Malacca, the main trade route to Singapore and the Far East, the issue subsided into farce as the exact location of these straits was debated by the two party leaders. *The Times* concluded that the question was more suited to a civil service examination paper. It was a blunder, for Disraeli was wrong in his claims and his geography. It was also Disraeli's sole attempt to beat the patriotic drum. He fell back on the charge that national institutions were not safe in Liberal hands, calling upon the electors to return to power a party who would maintain England's strength and 'support by every means her imperial sway'. The electors obliged and Disraeli formed his second (and last) government in February 1874, having secured a Conservative majority of forty-eight seats.

How far had Disraeli's imperial ideas advanced during the controversial years 1867–74? The answer must surely be not very much. He played little part in the Abyssinian expedition and, in any case, it is difficult to see this as heralding a new departure in imperial policy. There seems, therefore, to be no substance to the claim that he had already launched Britain on an aggressive new imperialism. He had not laid out a Conservative programme for the future nor had he once advocated imperial expansion. On the contrary, he had attacked Liberal intervention in West Africa. Nor had he shown any concern for the needs of the colonies during the controversy over Granville's colonial policy.

What had Disraeli done? Although his famous Crystal Palace speech merely reiterated ideas long held, two new concepts had been publicly added to the traditional Tory concern of defending national institutions — elevating the condition of the people and upholding the empire. Whether he had, as yet, successfully annexed the cause of empire to the Conservative party is doubtful. Nevertheless, in his speeches he had consistently portrayed the Conservative party as the 'national' or 'patriotic' party and he had linked patriotism with empire. A new creed was in the process of being fashioned around the monarchy, the landed settlement, the established Church, the empire and the nation. In the changing circumstances of Europe and the wider world, he had also called for a more active foreign policy, emphasizing the role that overseas possessions could play in assisting Great Britain on the world stage. As in 1833, the empire remained for Disraeli one of the main sources of Britain's greatness. It was now also the key to Britain's future as a world power. But all this was in the realm of rhetoric. Disraeli was about to assume power again and his reputation as a pioneer of the New Imperialism would stand or fall by the actions and ideas promoted during his last administration.

4. The Expansionist?

In 1878, after the triumphant return of Disraeli (now earl of Beaconsfield) from the Congress of Berlin, Gladstone launched into a long diatribe against Disraeli's claim to have secured 'Peace with Honour'. He began by attacking the recently negotiated occupation of Cyprus as symbolic of the government's expanding imperial appetite which had first swallowed up the Fiji Islands and then the Transvaal. 'Territorial aggrandisement, backed by military display', he wrote, had become the '*cheval de bataille*' of the administration. This attack heralded the beginning of an ideological battle over the character of the British empire which culminated in Gladstone's 1879–80 winter campaign in Midlothian. The setbacks in the Afghan and Zulu wars played into Gladstone's hands. The drawbacks of a government committed to a programme of aggression and imperial expansion, he thundered, were obvious in the expenditure of 'blood and treasure', mounting debt and higher taxes, which were impoverishing the British people.

In retrospect, it is easy to see how the rhetoric and policies of the 1874–80 administration earned for Disraeli the reputation of a reckless and warmongering advocate of imperial expansion. The government's record seemed to be one of feverish intervention overseas. Within a few months of the formation of the ministry, the Fiji Islands were annexed, British influence extended into the hinterland of the Gold Coast colony, and British residents, on the Indian model, installed as rulers in all but name in three of the western Malay States. The following year witnessed Disraeli's much publicized purchase of the Suez Canal Company shares, the launch of two confederation schemes — one in South Africa, the other in the West Indies — and a war in Perak. In 1876 riots occurred in Barbados and, amid a great deal of hostile publicity, the Queen was made Empress of India. A year later, the Transvaal Republic was annexed, British influence further extended in the Pacific Ocean by the creation of the Western Pacific High Commission, and Russia was threatened with war. In 1878 came the climax of the Eastern Question crisis with Disraeli's triumphant appearance at the Congress of Berlin, followed by the announcement of the British occupation of Cyprus. Finally, the ministry closed with the establishment of an Anglo-French 'dual control' in Egypt and the outbreak of wars in Afghanistan and Zululand, both involving dramatic early reversals of British fortunes. All this was accompanied by much high-flown rhetoric and bragging about the strength and glory of empire. Disraeli's contribution to both the expansion of the empire and the promotion of imperial ideology seemed incontestable and it is on the record of this ministry that his reputation as a pioneer of the New Imperialism mainly rests.

It must have come as a great surprise to the newly-appointed Cabinet that, despite Disraeli's inspiring speeches, the new prime minister did not seem to have any legislation in mind, let alone a prepared programme of reforms to hand. The Queen's Speech was consequently framed with some difficulty. It was a hand-to-mouth affair, typical of the man. Never interested in planning, always prepared to improvise, he was a politician of broad vision who could rarely be bothered with detail. This he willingly left to subordinates. Consequently, legislation tended to emerge in a rather piecemeal fashion, the work of individual ministers presided over by a prime minister whose presentational skills were deployed to give the appearance of a planned and coherent programme.

Disraeli lacked Gladstone's robust stamina. He had shown no inclination to oversee the work of his ministers in 1868 and was even less likely to do so now that he was an elderly widower of seventy in poor health. Nevertheless, he had not lost his deftness of touch or his imagination. He was still capable of flashes of brilliance and inspiration. Fortunately, he had assembled a talented team. He managed to entice Salisbury and Carnarvon back into the fold. His relationship with Salisbury improved dramatically after the latter's appointment as foreign secretary in 1878; his relationship with Carnarvon always remained distant and awkward. Relations with the younger Stanley, now fifteenth earl of Derby, a friend of long standing, also deteriorated as their views over the conduct of foreign policy diverged — in 1878 both Derby and Carnarvon resigned from the Cabinet.

As regards the empire, Disraeli had never shown much interest in colonial administration and had no wish to dictate colonial policy. It was the possession of empire, especially India, and the use to which it could be put in reinforcing Great Britain's role on the world scene, that interested him most. He frequently, therefore, took Salisbury, the secretary of state for India, into his confidence. He was happy to leave Carnarvon to his own devices.

Carnarvon served his apprenticeship in the Colonial Office as parliamentary under-secretary in 1858–9 and colonial secretary in 1866–7. He presided over the arrangements for the British North America Act creating the Dominion of Canada and headed the attack in the House of Lords on Granville's colonial policy in 1870. His main interests were good government, economy and imperial defence. Except where security was the prime concern, Carnarvon was not the man to favour annexation. The new foreign secretary, Derby, was an even more committed non-interventionist. Current economic conditions — trade depression, bad harvests and rising unemployment which caused the chancellor of the Exchequer increasing difficulties in his desperate battle to balance his budgets — also indicated that an expansionist policy was not in prospect. By 1880, the Liberal surplus of over five million pounds had been turned into a large deficit.

How then do we account for the feverish activity overseas during the years 1874–80? Did the election victory in 1874 really herald the implementation of a new Conservative philosophy of empire? Did the government intentionally follow a costly expansionist and aggressive policy overseas? Was Disraeli responsible for these developments and does he deserve to be called a pioneer of the New Imperialism? Not surprisingly, the record of this government has been closely scrutinized by historians of empire.

When Carnarvon took over the Colonial Office, he was faced with several urgent problems relating to the imperial frontier in the tropics. Required to take immediate decisions, the actions of the new colonial secretary, and the language he used to announce them, certainly seemed to confirm that a series of 'forward movements' were being undertaken in conformity with a new outlook on empire. Disraeli, however, showed little interest in these matters.

On the day the Liberals conceded defeat, news that the Ashanti king had sued for peace reached Britain. The victory was loudly acclaimed in the newspapers and the expedition's leader, Sir Garnet

Wolseley, became a popular hero. Carnarvon wisely warned his chief against attempting to gain further political capital out of the war. Faced with a 'very evil choice' about the future of the Gold Coast, the stark alternatives being withdrawal (as recommended by the West African select committee in 1865) or annexation of the area between the coast and Ashanti, the so-called 'protectorate' in which the Fante peoples lived, Carnarvon announced:

> A great nation like ours must be sometimes prepared to discharge disagreeable duties; she must consent to bear burdens which are inseparable from her greatness . . . it is certainly not a desire of selfish interests or the ambition of larger empire which bids us remain on the West Coast of Africa; it is simply and solely a sense of obligations to be redeemed and of duties to be performed. (3 Hansard 219: 157, 168)

Despite the grandeur of the words, the policy was mild enough: the Gold Coast forts were added to the island of Lagos to form a new Crown colony which was later empowered to legislate for the protectorate. Thus, British authority was extended without acquiring additional territory. The only real innovation was the result of a hostile motion by philanthropists in the House of Commons calling for the abolition of domestic slavery on the coast. Disraeli obliged Carnarvon to reopen the question and, having passed the final responsibility to the man on the spot, Carnarvon received all the bouquets when a proclamation ending domestic slavery was accepted quietly. Disraeli's report was glowing: 'It is a masterly, indeed admirable performance, your conduct of your office cannot be too highly praised.'

Of even greater concern were events in the South Pacific. Increasing lawlessness in the Fiji Islands, especially among Europeans, together with escalating demands from the American government for compensation for earlier incidents involving American citizens, had already led Cakobau, the self-proclaimed Tui Viti ('king of all Fiji') to offer the islands to Queen Victoria on two occasions in the 1850s. Now that an additional problem of labour recruiting ('blackbirding' or the 'kidnapping' trade, as it was called at the time) had hit the headlines with the murder of Bishop Patteson of Melanesia in 1871, annexation seemed to be the only answer. Gladstone, however, had objected. Instead, two commissioners, Commodore J. Goodenough and Consul Edgar Layard, were appointed to investigate the situation. Their report was still awaited when the Liberals left office.

As so frequently happened, commissioners sent to inquire and report acted first and reported afterwards. Despite a hurried telegram from Carnarvon advising caution, Goodenough and Layard engineered a third offer of cession in March 1874. When their report finally arrived three months later, Carnarvon found that he had been presented with a virtual *fait accompli*. Announcing in the Lords, on 17 July 1874, that provided an unqualified offer of cession could be obtained the offer would not be denied, he stated: 'I hardly like to say that England has a mission to extend her policy of colonisation in this part of the world, but at all events it does seem to me that there is an indirect duty which lies upon us . . .'

Carnarvon was infuriated by Disraeli's subsequent refusal to hold a Cabinet meeting to discuss the matter. Fearing his ministry might collapse following contentious debates concerning the Public Worship Regulation Bill, which the High Church Salisbury and Carnarvon had attacked in the Lords, Disraeli responded to Carnarvon's veiled threat of resignation in August 1874 by telling him:

> It was most unlucky that we were obliged to put off the Cabinet — but it was your vote, and perhaps speech, that occasioned that, for if I had not worked from the moment I rose until noon, the Commons would have rebelled . . . However, I must leave the matter entirely to your discretion. There is none of my colleagues in whom I have more confidence than yourself, and I always say that your administration of your office is most able. (Arthur Hardinge, *Life of Henry Howard Molyneaux Herbert, Fourth Earl of Carnarvon, 1831–1890* (London, Humphrey Milford, Oxford University Press, 1925), vol.II, 74)

Thus, the Fiji Islands were added to the empire in October 1874 at the 'discretion' of the colonial secretary. Disraeli's verdict was that Carnarvon was 'very busy annexing provinces to the Empire' and 'seems to be distinguishing himself'.

Carnarvon did, indeed, have his hands full. A further extension of British influence occurred in the Malay States. Here, another delicate situation had been inherited from the Liberals. Civil wars in two of the western Malay States, Perak and Selangor, in which Chinese miners had joined in the dynastic disputes of the Malay rulers, and unrest in the neighbouring state of Sungei Ujong, had badly affected the tin trade, led to piratical attacks on British shipping in the Straits of Malacca, and threatened the security of the Straits Settlements colony (Penang, Malacca and Singapore). The

Liberal colonial secretary instructed Governor Sir Andrew Clarke to investigate the advisability of appointing British advisers to the Malay rulers. Once again the man on the spot exceeded his instructions, arranging political settlements in the three states and securing the appointment of residents. Left to deal with this insubordination, Carnarvon could do little. Without informing the Cabinet, he eventually gave a conditional approval to the new system. Clarke's successor, however, proved even more headstrong and tried to turn the resident advisers into virtual rulers. The result was, first, a skirmish in Sungei Ujong in December 1874, and then, following the murder of the impetuous British resident, a full-scale war in Perak which necessitated an expedition as large as that used against Ashanti. Disraeli, busy purchasing the Suez Canal Company shares, was soon obliged to pay closer attention to events. On his advice a proclamation was issued repudiating annexation and announcing occupation with a view to obtaining indemnity. Fortunately, the crisis passed without further mishap.

Were these 'forward movements' in the tropics part of a new expansionist Conservative philosophy of empire allegedly fore-shadowed in Disraeli's Crystal Palace speech? Nothing could be further from the truth. In each region a policy of limited involvement had been adopted, extensions of authority, not territory, being the order of the day. Even the annexation of Fiji was treated as an experiment in Pacific island government: proposals to annex Rotuma, Samoa and New Guinea were rapidly quashed. And when it proved necessary to extend British jurisdiction in order to regulate the recruitment of Polynesian labourers, the Western Pacific High Commission was created, thereby extending consular powers to the governor of Fiji and avoiding annexation of further territory. Having inherited these problems from the Liberals, Carnarvon did little more, despite his fine language, than carry out the intentions of his predecessor. The 1874 election made little difference to policy in these regions. And Disraeli's role in it all was virtually nil.

The same is true of the West Indies and South Africa, where Carnarvon launched his confederation schemes in 1875. Neither scheme was new — Kimberley had tried to implement confederation in both regions — and neither was expansionist in intent. Consolidation was the aim, creating larger, administratively more efficient and economical units, better able to stand on their own feet, to defend themselves, and attract officials of high calibre. The Leeward Islands in the West Indies had been successfully federated in 1871. Carnarvon decided to appoint a more energetic governor in Barbados to complete the process in the Windward Islands. Unfortunately, Sir John Pope Hennessy's actions alarmed the white planters and aroused undue hopes in the populace. Riots ensued at Easter 1876. All prospect of federation was then at an end and the governor had to be diplomatically transferred to Hong Kong in 1877. Disraeli did not intervene.

This was but a curtain-raiser to an even worse failure in South Africa, a key area in the empire's defence network. The Cape retained its importance as 'the tavern' on the route to India. Here, the security as well as the prosperity of the British possessions — Cape Colony, Natal, Griqualand West and Basutoland — were being threatened by the presence in the interior of two unstable Boer republics — the Orange Free State and the Transvaal — forever searching for an independent outlet to the sea, attacking or being attacked by various African peoples and, in the process, giving rise to the fear of a general African uprising. In addition, the generally inefficient and uneconomic administration of these colonies and republics and their mutual jealousies and petty differences harmed the trade and commerce of the region. Federation, again, seemed the logical answer.

In May 1875, following a minor rebellion in the north of Natal, Carnarvon decided the time was ripe to revive Kimberley's earlier scheme. Derby noted that the plan was 'sharply criticized, and I think that no member of the Cabinet quite likes it'. In fact, conditions for a spontaneous federation did not exist. The Boer republics had no wish to come under British domination once again and the Cape Colony objected to carrying the debts and defence burdens of poorer states. Carnarvon's heavy-handed approach, along with the employment of an undiplomatic personal envoy, J. A. Froude, alienated the colonists further. A last-ditch attempt to salvage the scheme by assembling a conference in London ended in abject failure. Carnarvon concluded that pressure would have to be brought on the two Boer republics.

An opportunity arose in the summer of 1876 when the Transvaal, verging on bankruptcy, suffered a series of setbacks in skirmishes with one of its African peoples and the Zulus and Swazis seemed to be adopting an aggressive stance on its borders. Carnarvon sought Disraeli's permission to send Sir Theophilus Shepstone to prevail on the Boers to accept British rule:

> My hope is that by acting at once, we may prevent war and acquire at
> a stroke the whole of the Transvaal Republic, after which the Orange
> Free State will follow, and the whole policy in South Africa, for which
> we have been labouring [will be] fully and completely justified.
> (Monypenny and Buckle, op. cit., vol.VI (1920), 414)

Disraeli showed little concern. Far from taking a close interest in the
proceedings, or being intent on initiating an aggressive, expansionist
scheme, the prime minister responded in a very casual fashion: 'In all
these affairs I must trust to you, and you are a person in whom I have
much trust. Do what you think wisest.' The Transvaal was added to
the empire in April 1877 without the Cabinet even being consulted.

Unfortunately the colonial secretary had blundered. The Boers of
the Transvaal soon regretted their hasty action in agreeing to
annexation and remained disaffected. The British had also inherited
a border dispute with the Zulus that rapidly threatened to get out of
hand. By the time Carnarvon resigned in 1878, Disraeli was only too
aware of the enormity of 'Twitters' blunders':

> if anything annoys me more than another it is our Cape affairs, where
> every day brings forward a new blunder of Twitters.
>
> The man he swore by was Sir T. Shepstone, whom he looked upon
> as heaven-born for the object in view. We sent him out entirely for
> Twitters' sake, and he has managed to quarrel with English, Dutch,
> and Zulus — and now he is obliged to be recalled; but not before he
> has brought on, I fear, a new war. Froude was bad enough, and had
> cost us a million, this will be worse. So much for Twitters. (Marquis of
> Zetland (ed.), *The Letters of Disraeli to Lady Bradford and Lady
> Chesterfield* (London, Ernest Benn, 1929), vol.II, 189)

In January 1878, Carnarvon warned Sir Bartle Frere, his newly
appointed governor of the Cape Colony and high commissioner for
South Africa, that the time was inopportune for a South African war.
Frere, one of the most forceful pro-consuls of his day, believed that
the power of the Zulus would have to be broken if the internal
security of British possessions were to be assured. He needed to be
kept on a tight rein. Unfortunately, Carnarvon's successor, Sir
Michael Hicks Beach, had no previous acquaintance with colonial
affairs and did not realize, until too late, that Frere's determination
to assert British paramountcy south of the Zambesi was leading to
the complications the British government feared most. Hicks Beach
hurriedly warned the governor to abandon plans for a preventive

war. Frere, however, defiantly went ahead with his ultimatum to the Zulu king and war ensued in January 1879, bringing with it that greatest of defeats inflicted on a British army by an African people. The news of Isandlwana shook the nation and Gladstone had a field day criticizing Disraeli's aggressive and expansionist imperial policy.

But concurrent wars against the Afghans and Zulus were the last thing Disraeli wanted. Privately he believed Frere 'ought to be impeached'. But since Hicks Beach and the Queen vehemently supported Frere, he bowed to their pressure and, in public, resisted all demands for his recall. Thus, Disraeli's name became associated in South Africa with an expansionist policy in the Transvaal to which he had paid little attention and a war against the Zulus which he had opposed. Far from being the product of an aggressive intent, the Zulu war was the product of Disraeli's weakness as prime minister; his failure to oversee ministers and control men on the spot led to costly, unforeseen and unwanted complications. His public defence of Frere, however, convinced many contemporaries and several generations of historians that he was a warmonger intent on a policy of aggressive expansion overseas.

Disraeli played little part in the formulation of colonial policy. He certainly did not have the insatiable greed for territory that Gladstone alleged and he remained decidedly averse to the annexation of Ashanti, the Malay states and Zululand. He had little interest in Africa and the tropics and his contribution to policy was largely negative — nothing more than a few letters of encouragement to a difficult colleague. Nor was the policy of Carnarvon one of imperial expansion. In the West Indies and South Africa consolidation was his watchword. In the tropics he followed a policy of minimum intervention. True, things did go wrong and some expansion did occur, but it was not part of a new Conservative philosophy of empire and was certainly not presided over by Disraeli. Even when Carnarvon was keen to restore the British garrisons overseas and Disraeli assured him of the prime minister's support,

> I look upon the restoration of our military relations with our Colonies as a question of high policy, which ought never to be absent from our thoughts. The question involves social and political, as well as military considerations; and you may rely on my earnest support of any steps on your part to accomplish this great end . . . (Hardinge, op. cit., II, 98)

Disraeli did nothing to promote a policy about which he had spoken so much in the past. Carnarvon's project was subsequently throttled in Cabinet by the secretary of state for war with Treasury support.

Colonial administration had never been of deep concern to Disraeli. It was the idea of empire, India and the East which fired his imagination. Perhaps, then, it is on those activities outside the Colonial Office's sphere that Disraeli's reputation as an expansionist and pioneer of the New Imperialism rests. After all, the purchase of the Suez Canal Company shares, the Royal Titles Bill, the occupation of Cyprus, and, to a lesser extent, the establishment of the Anglo-French dual control in Egypt, are all much more clearly associated with Disraeli's name. And what of Disraeli's policies in India? Did he inaugurate a more aggressive policy which came to a climax in the second and third Afghan wars? Here there is likely to be a much more fruitful line of enquiry.

The purchase of 176,602 Suez Canal Company shares in November 1875 was one of those sudden diplomatic and personal coups in which Disraeli revelled. Hearing that the virtually bankrupt Egyptian khedive was negotiating with a French syndicate the sale of his last remaining asset, Disraeli convinced the Cabinet that control of this important seaway could not be allowed to fall entirely into French hands. Arrangements were immediately made with Lionel de Rothschild to raise £4,000,000 to buy the shares which amounted to a holding of 44 per cent of the original issue. Disraeli may have trumpeted to the Queen, 'It is just settled: you have it, Madam', and 'The Faery' may have been in ecstasies, but the event needs to be kept in perspective. Forty-four per cent was not a controlling interest and the voting rights on the shares had already been mortgaged until 1895 (and even then carried a maximum of only ten votes). The company did not control the canal and could not 'shut it up': freedom of passage was assured by an international guarantee.

Nor did Disraeli wish for any further advance in Egypt. It was not simply that he wished to retain French co-operation. The answer to those who said England should take Egypt to safeguard her route to India was obvious:

> If the Russians had Constantinople, they could at any time march their Army through Syria to the mouth of the Nile, and then what would be the use of our holding Egypt? Not even the command of the

sea could help us under such circumstances. People who talk in this manner must be utterly ignorant of geography . . . Constantinople is the key of India, not Egypt and the Suez Canal. (Monypenny and Buckle, op. cit., VI (1920), 84)

The outbreak of the Russo-Turkish war in 1877 led to numerous suggestions that Britain should annex Egypt, but the government resisted such an idea — and Disraeli ignored a similar suggestion from Bismarck during the Congress of Berlin. Even when the khedive dismissed his English and French ministers in 1879, and it looked as if the use of force might be necessary, international pressure was used on the sultan of Turkey to ensure the replacement of the khedive and the establishment of the 'dual control'. Disraeli fought shy of further involvement in Egypt, especially as the British army was fully occupied in South Africa.

By this time Disraeli had achieved another notable personal success: by a secret Anglo-Turkish convention prior to the Congress of Berlin, it was agreed that in return for a defensive alliance and safeguards for the sultan's Christian subjects in Asia Minor, England would occupy and administer Cyprus to counteract proposed Russian gains elsewhere. While all the planning and spadework was undoubtedly done by Salisbury, it was Disraeli who took all the credit. It was one of those daring innovatory acts which caused a sensation, especially as it was announced after a flurry of criticism concerning the leaked news of the Russian acquisition of Batum and Kars. Disraeli milked the situation to the full. 'Cyprus is the key of Western Asia,' he told the Queen. Its acquisition would strengthen British power in the eastern Mediterranean and 'weld together Your Majesty's Indian Empire and Great Britain'. In the House of Lords, he stated: 'In taking Cyprus the movement is not Mediterranean, it is Indian.' It was for the preservation of the empire and of peace. Whether Cyprus ever added anything to Britain's imperial defence system has always been hotly disputed.

India was certainly at the centre of Disraeli's imperial ideas. It is the scene of the last alleged acts of aggressive, expansionist policy mentioned earlier: the second and third Afghan wars. Were these the result of a new aggressive Conservative philosophy or were they the result of muddled policy, an incompetent secretary of state and a disobedient viceroy?

India was economically, militarily, and in terms of prestige by far the most important of Great Britain's overseas possessions. It received about one-fifth of Britain's total overseas investments and a similar quantity of British exports. Import and export duties were also manipulated to Britain's advantage. India's surplus of trade with the Far East financed the deficit in British trade to that region. Every imaginable expense associated with governing India was charged to the Indian taxpayer. In addition, India was the base for British power in the eastern hemisphere. The Indian army had often been used as the long arm of the British empire in Afghanistan, Burma, Persia, China, New Zealand and Abyssinia. India was one of the keys to Britain's greatness. Disraeli knew all this and was determined to exploit Britain's advantages to the full.

Not surprisingly, the new ministry adopted a more self-interested and forceful policy towards India than that of the Liberals. Salisbury's plans included a reduction of tariffs on British cotton goods, circumscription of the vernacular press and a lowering of the maximum age of entry into the Indian civil service to eighteen, thereby making it more difficult for Indian recruits to gain admission. The major change was in external policy: a shift away from 'masterly inactivity' in favour of a more forward policy in order to counteract the steady advance of Russia across central Asia. There was now a hostile major power virtually on the northern frontier of India. The viceroy, Lord Northbrook, was instructed in January 1875 to secure the appointment of British agents at Herat within the amir of Afghanistan's territories. The ensuing exchange of views and Northbrook's subsequent resignation, ostensibly for personal reasons, revealed how far the Conservatives had decided to depart from previous Liberal policy.

When the volatile Lord Lytton was appointed viceroy in 1876, Disraeli acknowledged that 'we wanted a man of ambition, imagination, some vanity and much will — and we have got him'. No time was lost in secretly instructing Lytton to persuade the amir to accept resident British agents. The amir, having been rebuffed by the previous administration, refused to co-operate. Consequently, when an unheralded Russian mission suddenly arrived in Kabul, Lytton resolved to send a British mission as well. The Cabinet advised caution but Lytton went ahead and ordered the British mission to enter Afghanistan. It was turned back at the frontier and war ensued. Disraeli was furious with Lytton:

> He was told to wait until we had received the answer from Russia to our remonstrance . . . He was told to send the Mission by Candahar.

He has sent it by the Khyber, and received a snub, wh. it may cost us much to wipe away.

When V-Roys and Comms.-in-chief disobey orders, they ought to be sure of success in their mutiny. Lytton by disobeying orders, has only secured insult and failure . . . To force the Khyber, and take Cabul, is a perilous business. (Monypenny and Buckle, op. cit., VI (1920), 382)

In public, however, the prime minister supported the rebellious viceroy and talked grandly of securing a 'scientific frontier'.

At first all went well: after a model campaign, the Afghans were defeated and a treaty was made giving Britain control over three frontier districts and two passes, including the Khyber. A British mission was also installed in Kabul. Unfortunately, just as the viceroy's actions seemed to be vindicated, another 'shaker' (as Disraeli called it) hit the government: the mission was wiped out during a five-hour attack by mutinous Afghan soldiers. A second campaign had to be fought and Gladstone added yet another indictment to his list of Disraeli's misguided and extravagant ventures abroad.

Yet Disraeli had never made any plans for an Afghan war and a good case has been made (Cowling 1961) that it was once again the weakness of the prime minister — a failure to oversee Cabinet ministers, to control men on the spot, and an unwillingness to admit that developments did not spring from decided policy — that was the real cause of the mess. But the disobedient viceroy was not the sole culprit. The secretary of state for India, Earl Cranbrook, was particularly incompetent in not informing Lytton of the decision to wait until a response to the diplomatic protest was received from St Petersburg and in not making it clear that an approach through the Khyber pass was forbidden. Disraeli must also bear a larger share of the responsibility in this case. In the week before his outburst about mutinous viceroys, he wrote twice to Cranbrook: 'With Lytton's general policy I entirely agree. I have always been opposed to, and deplored, "masterly inactivity" . . . there shd be no delay in the Mission', and:

when you and the V-roy agree I shall as a general rule, always wish to support you.

No doubt Salisbury's views, under ordinary circumstances, would be prudent; but there are occasions when prudence is not wisdom.

And this is one. There are times for action. We must control and even create events . . . what we want, at this present moment, is to prove our ascendancy in Afghanistan, and to accomplish that, we must not stick at trifles. (Monypenny and Buckle, op. cit., 381–2)

When a British mission was finally installed in Kabul, he was delighted at the successful implementation of Lytton's original instructions: 'We have secured a scientific and adequate frontier for our Indian empire . . . whatever happens it will always be to me of real satisfaction that I had the opportunity of placing you on the throne of the Great Moghul.' Disraeli, even though he did not want war, bears more responsibility than was once thought. However, even on the north-west frontier Disraeli did not follow a decidedly expansionist policy. The acquisitions in the Treaty of Gandamak were comparatively minor, given his talk of a 'scientific frontier', and he also urged against further annexation following the second campaign.

Did this amount to a policy of 'territorial aggrandisement, backed by military display'? Elsewhere in the empire there had been no grandiose policy of expansion in the tropics. Policy in the West Indies and South Africa had also been consolidationist in intent, although some expansion did incur. Even the dramatic purchase of the Suez Canal Company shares and the occupation of Cyprus were basically attempts to prevent France stealing a march in Egypt and Russia in Asia Minor. Disraeli was not the expansionist he is so frequently alleged to have been.

There was little ground for Gladstone's accusation of the deliberate adoption of a costly and unnecessary policy of blatant 'imperialism'. As P. R. Ghosh noted: 'The extremity of the Liberal indictment of "Beaconsfieldism" became incredible as soon as it was successful.' And yet people believed it at the time. Even Cabinet colleagues commented on the gap between Disraeli's actual policies and the grandiose purposes they were supposed to serve. D. C. Gordon was surely correct when he wrote of the 'histrionic embrace which Disraeli extended to the idea of expansion'. Perhaps he was also right when he insisted that 'Disraeli's imperialism was essentially rhetorical'. Lord Blake highlighted the importance of distinguishing presentation from policy when dealing with Disraeli, and it has frequently been suggested that Disraeli's contribution to the long-term fortunes of the Conservative party owed much more to ideas, slogans, rhetoric and presentation than to specific policies and actual legislation. No assessment of Disraeli's contribution to the character of British imperialism and the onset of the New Imperialism would be complete without examining Disraeli's rhetoric and the romantic ideas contained in his speeches.

5.   The Romantic?

Following Beaconsfield's triumphant return from the Congress of Berlin proclaiming 'peace with honour', the *Spectator* recorded in July 1878:

> If the shrewdest political thinker in England had been told thirty years ago that the bizarre and flashy novelist, who had just given the world *Coningsby*, *Sybil* and *Tancred*, would within a generation be not only ruling England, but ruling England on the lines of the ideas set forth in that very extraordinary series of political primers . . . we cannot doubt that the shrewd political thinker we have supposed would have treated such a prophecy as the raving of a lunatic. Yet that is exactly what has happened. (G. C. Thompson, *Public Opinion and Lord Beaconsfield, 1875–1880* (London, Macmillan, 1886), vol.II, 479–80)

Disraeli was nothing if not a showman. His theatricality, his penchant for flamboyant gestures and his extravagant political rhetoric were used to good effect during his second ministry. As a result, contemporaries often confused the rhetoric of Conservative policy with its reality.

Disraeli's image also owes much to the propaganda of his opponents, especially to Gladstone's depiction of 'Beaconsfieldism' and his portrayal of Disraeli as a new Machiavelli intent on undermining British political liberties and sacrificing the well-being and progress of the British people. In December 1879, he recorded in his diary that for the past three and a half years he had been passing through 'a political experience which I believe is without example in our Parliamentary history'. The battle to be fought was 'a battle of justice, humanity, freedom, law, . . . all on a gigantic scale'.

While Disraeli's ambition, personality and rhetoric undoubtedly led many to fear his intentions, the accusations were certainly heightened by the deep personal antagonism of the two principal combatants, their differing views on empire, and their soaring passions as the duel progressed, often to the dismay of their adherents. 'Gladstone and Dizzy seem to cap one another in folly and pretence, and I don't know which has made the greatest ass of himself,' Harcourt wailed, as both leaders vacated the middle ground traditionally occupied by the majority of their supporters. Thus developed the great contest of the late 1870s, with Disraeli charged with wishing to practise 'autocratic' imperialism at home and abroad.

The Conservative election manifesto had criticized the Liberal government's lack of energy in foreign policy and promised instead to maintain England's strength and 'support by every means her imperial sway'. Disraeli lost no opportunity to return to his imperial rhetoric of earlier years. He also sought an early opportunity to restore Britain to the ranks of the great powers by the spirited promotion of British national interests in Europe and beyond. While he remained uncertain exactly how to achieve this, 'peace' and 'empire' were soon adopted as the twin justifications of his foreign policy.

At the lord mayor's luncheons in the Guildhall in November 1874 and 1875, Disraeli proclaimed his pride in empire, attacked the Liberals for their past lack of faith in the colonies, and declared his intention to 'consolidate and confirm' imperial relationships. His first real opportunity to beat the patriotic drum came with that 'high-class piece of cloak and dagger work': the purchase of the Suez Canal Company shares. From this time on, the 'Eastern Empire' dominated Disraeli's imperial and foreign policies. Disraeli maintained that the purchase of the Suez Canal Company shares was in the interests of the empire:

> Some may take an economical view of the subject, some may take a commercial view, some may take a peaceful view, some may take a warlike view of it; but of this I feel persuaded — and I speak with confidence — that when I appeal to the House of Commons for their vote they will agree with the country, that this was a purchase which was necessary to maintain the Empire, and which favours in every degree the policy which this country ought to sustain. (3 *Hansard* 227: 102)

And again:

> I have always and do now recommend it to the country as a political

transaction, and one which I believe is calculated to strengthen the Empire. That is the spirit in which it has been accepted by the country . . . They are really seasick of the 'Silver Streak'. They want the Empire to be maintained, to be strengthened. They will not be alarmed even if it be increased. (Ibid., 661)

Disraeli used much more flamboyant language in his speeches defending the Royal Titles Bill. The decision to make the Queen Empress of India was certainly in line with his imperial ideas and it was also intended as a warning to Russia of British intentions in India. But Disraeli was not happy with the timing. It is clear that the Queen herself urged the introduction of the bill — 'The Empress-Queen demands her Imperial Crown', Disraeli told Cairns — and he instructed Salisbury to place a paragraph in the Queen's Speech following a reference to the prince of Wales's visit to India so that 'What may have been looked upon as an ebullition of individual vanity may bear the semblance of deep and organised policy'.

Unfortunately the Royal Titles Bill ran into heavy storms. While the assumption of the imperial title had been mooted since the proclamation of British rule in 1858, opposition to the alien nature and continental associations of the title of 'empress' was unexpectedly strong. In response, Disraeli made a series of impressive rhetorical speeches in which his picture of the Indian masses clamouring to pay homage not to a distant suzerain but to their very own empress was as convincing as his description of the British colonist who 'finds a nugget' or 'fleeces a thousand flocks' before returning home to live in rich retirement — a romantic concept, which had little basis in reality. **[DOCUMENT VIII]** Eventually the bill was passed out of deference to the known wishes of the Queen.

It was during this debate that the press first adopted the word 'imperialism' (to underline the alien character of the new title) as an anti-Disraeli slogan. The *Spectator*, on 8 April 1876, in an article entitled 'English Imperialism', commented:

It is not easy to realise that such a policy as that of the 'Imperialists', as they are called on the Continent, should have, we will not say any root, but even any possibility of root, in these islands. Yet it is evident that Mr Disraeli conceived very early in his career the notion that such a policy, — a policy which should magnify the Crown on one hand, and the wishes of the masses on the other, and should make light of the constitutional limitations on either, — was still possible in Europe, and might even have a chance in England . . .

Once again, controversy and criticism had been aroused by a prime minister not fully in control of events.

While Disraeli's 'hyperbolic historical fantasy' and the elaborate ceremonial in India, devised by the poet-viceroy Lord Lytton, to accompany the transformation of the absent Queen into an empress, established Disraeli's reputation as an exponent of the romantic imperial ideal and began the association of the Conservative party with the empire in the public imagination, much had also been said and written about the dangers which Disraeli's actions posed to English constitutional usage. It was Disraeli's actions and speeches during the Eastern Question crisis, however, which fuelled the controversies surrounding 'imperialism' and led to the word becoming a hostile political slogan in the election of 1880.

Disraeli returned to office determined to restore Great Britain's position in the councils of Europe. The Franco-Prussian war and the 'German revolution', he maintained, had destroyed the existing balance of power. He therefore aimed to restore the European 'equilibrium' and remove the shackles on Britain's functioning as a great power. How this was to be done he seems to have had little idea. No doubt something would turn up.

It was the continuing decline of the Ottoman empire which provided Disraeli with his first opportunity to flex his muscles on the European stage. The traditional Palmerstonian strategy which Disraeli inherited was to support Turkey in order to prevent Russia from becoming a Mediterranean power by acquiring Constantinople or gaining access through the Balkans. Another fear was Russian acquisition of territory in Asia Minor which would permit an advance on the Red Sea or the Persian Gulf. Russia had already extended her empire across central Asia towards the northern border of India. Disraeli's strategy, therefore, was to detach Russia from Austria-Hungary and Germany and take an independent line in European affairs concerning Turkey. Disraeli's Indian and oriental interests and his desire to restore British prestige in Europe came together in the unfolding Eastern Question crisis.

In July 1875, a series of minor revolts began in Herzegovina which spread to other Christian provinces in the Ottoman empire. The misgovernment of the Porte was notorious. Russia, Germany and Austria-Hungary immediately demanded Turkish governmental reforms. Disraeli's government, however, intent on looking after Britain's imperial interests, of which Turkey was a natural prop, and intent, too, on striking a blow at the Dreikaiserbund, acted coolly towards the proposals of the three powers (the Andrassy Note and the Berlin Memorandum). The British fleet was even dispatched to Besika Bay near the southern entrance to the Dardanelles as a sign of support for Turkey. The government was greatly embarrassed, therefore, when news broke in June 1876 of the alleged massacre of some 25,000 Christian peasants in Bulgaria by Turkish irregular troops. Not surprisingly, the Conservative government was accused of supporting Muslim repression of Christian peoples in the Balkans.

Disraeli, not much concerned with humanitarian and religious issues when British interests were at stake, at first tried to dismiss the question of 'atrocities' (some of his remarks were thought to be flippant). In the last debate of the session, on 11 August 1876, he conceded that a massacre had occurred but denied that it warranted a change in British foreign policy. He concluded:

> those who suppose that England ever would uphold, or at this moment particularly is upholding, Turkey from blind superstition, and from a want of sympathy with the highest aspirations of humanity, are deceived. What our duty is at this critical moment is to maintain the Empire of England. Nor will we agree to any step, though it may obtain for a moment comparative quiet and a false prosperity, that hazards the existence of that Empire. (Monypenny and Buckle, op. cit., VI, 48)

The following day, Disraeli's elevation to the House of Lords as earl of Beaconsfield was announced. Appropriately enough, in the light of his subsequent reputation, 'empire' was the last word to pass his lips in the House of Commons.

On 6 September 1876, Gladstone emerged from retirement with his best-selling pamphlet, *The Bulgarian Horrors and the Question of the East*, which attacked Beaconsfield's policy. From this time on the old rivalry of Gladstone and Disraeli occupied centre-stage, Gladstone preaching a moral crusade and Disraeli parading 'national interests'. Thus, when Russia declared war on Turkey in April 1877, Beaconsfield immediately reverted to the traditional Palmerstonian strategy of defending Turkish territorial integrity. Despite the arguments of Salisbury and Northcote to the contrary, Disraeli genuinely seems to have believed that whoever held Constantinople could threaten the Suez Canal and hence the route to India. Gladstone, ignoring the advice of the Liberal leadership, attacked the government during the 'Five Nights' Debate' on the Eastern Question in May 1877: it was the beginning of a concerted attack on Disraeli's conduct of foreign affairs.

During the parliamentary recess, Gladstone became further embroiled in a heated exchange of views with Edward Dicey, the editor of the *Observer*, on the value of empire. In two articles in the *Nineteenth Century*, Dicey called for a British occupation of Egypt to forestall a Russian move into the Mediterranean. Britain should not shrink from further extending her territory in order to protect her existing possessions. Empire was part of Britain's 'manifest destiny'. Gladstone replied in no uncertain terms that empire was a burden of honour and a national weakness. Britain's only interest in India was the well-being of India. India 'does not add to but takes from our military strength': 'The root and pith and substance of the material greatness of our nation lies within the compass of these islands, and is, except in trifling particulars, independent of all and every sort of political Dominion beyond them.' The government's duty was to restrain the national instinct for empire.

Dicey retaliated by pouring scorn on the leader of the 'anti-imperialist theory of English statecraft'. Although the British empire had brought great benefit to mankind, basically it was for the sole benefit of the British. We ruled India 'because we deem the possession of India conducive to our interests and our reputation, because we have got it and intend to keep it'. **[DOCUMENT IX]** Dicey became 'the literary spokesman of an Empire spirit which was illiberal and militant, a spirit which the political crisis in the Near East had helped to hatch' (R. Koebner and H. Schmidt, *Imperialism: The Story and Significance of a Political Word, 1840–1960* (Cambridge, Cambridge University Press, 1964), 133). Indeed, as the Russians advanced towards Constantinople, that spirit was openly manifested on the streets, in working-class meetings and, above all, in the music hall. Beaconsfield's private secretary, Montagu Corry, reported that a recent by-election at Salford had 'turned on the Foreign question, mainly . . . the working class is neither for Russia, nor for Turkey, but thoroughly excited at the prospect of the interests or honour of England being touched . . . *In general*, I feel assured that Lancashire is determined that England shall not kiss the feet of Russia.' In May 1877, Corry went to the London Pavilion 'to feel the pulse of the holiday-makers': there was a song, very badly sung, but 'tumultuously cheered' at the end of each verse, because of the 'refrain':

> We'll give the Russian bear
> A taste of what we are,
> And fight to keep our empire of the seas.

[DOCUMENT X]

Within the space of a few months, the language of patriotism had been hijacked and attached to the defence of 'national interests'.

Disraeli was keen to turn such popular xenophobia to advantage. The major obstacle was his own Cabinet and, in particular, the obstruction of his foreign secretary, Lord Derby. In complete disarray, the best they could hope for was a façade of unity. Far from having a decided policy, Salisbury concluded: 'English policy is to float lazily down-stream, occasionally putting out a diplomatic boat-hook to avoid collision.' Disraeli was all for resolute action to prevent Russia from seizing the straits. As the prospect of war grew closer, Parliament was asked for a £6 million vote of credit, a British fleet was sent to Constantinople and an expeditionary force under Lord Napier of Magdala proposed. Such plans were too much for Carnarvon who promptly resigned. When the terms of the Treaty of San Stefano became known, endorsing Russian gains in the Balkans and Armenia, it became clear that, through her influence over Albania and an enlarged Bulgaria, Russia would become a Mediterranean power. Disraeli declared the empire to be in danger. He therefore proposed that a British expeditionary force should sail secretly from India to seize a *place d'armes* — Cyprus or Alexandretta — in the eastern Mediterranean. Derby now resigned. It was also decided to call up the reserves 'for the maintenance of peace and for the protection of the interests of the empire'.

In announcing this in the House of Lords on 8 April 1878, Disraeli returned to the rhetoric of his Royal Titles Bill speeches:

> I have ever considered that Her Majesty's Government of whatever Party formed, are the trustees of that Empire! That Empire was formed by the enterprise and energy of your ancestors, my Lords; and it is one of a very remarkable character. I know no example of it, either in ancient or modern history. No Caesar or Charlemagne ever presided over a Dominion so peculiar. Its flag floats on many waters; it has Provinces in every zone, they are inhabited by persons of different races, with different religions, different laws, manners, customs. Some of these are bound to us by the tie of liberty, fully conscious that

without their connection with the Metropolis they have no security for public freedom and self-government. Others united to us by faith and blood are influenced by material as well as moral considerations. There are millions who are bound to us by military sway, and they bow to that sway because they know that they are indebted to it for order and justice. But, my Lords, all these communities agree in recognising the commanding spirit of these Islands that has formed and fashioned in such a manner so great a portion of the globe. (3 *Hansard* 239: 777)

The speech foreshadowed the announcement, a week later, of the dispatch of 7,000 Indian troops to Malta.

Such brinkmanship caused tremendous excitement in both Parliament and the country. The rushing of Indian troops through the Suez Canal was the sort of bold and imaginative act that Disraeli delighted in. He told Queen Victoria:

After all the sneers of our not having any great military force, the imagination of the Continent will be much affected by the first appearance of what they will believe to be an inexhaustible supply of men . . . All that Lord Beaconsfield devised and contemplated, will now be carried into effect, and England already occupies again a leading and soon a commanding position. (Monypenny and Buckle, op. cit., VI, 285–6)

The constitutional legitimacy of the move was debated for three nights in the Commons in May 1878. The government was accused of violating the Bill of Rights. The movement of Indian troops had occurred at the behest of the British prime minister without the sanction of Parliament. It was a dangerous precedent. What was to stop an unscrupulous government using Asiatic troops to garrison London in the future? While the government escaped censure, the suspicion remained that Disraeli was trying to create a centralized, military empire beyond the normal constitutional safeguards.

The suspicion that the government was prepared to bypass Parliament was not diminished when the provisions of the Treaty of Berlin became known, including the military alliance with Turkey and the occupation of Cyprus. Additional far-reaching commitments had been entered into without the knowledge of Parliament. Worse, the new military concept of empire had been flaunted before a gullible British public. On his return from Berlin, Disraeli addressed the House of Lords in his best histrionic style:

Her Majesty has Fleets and Armies which are second to none. England must have seen with pride the Mediterranean covered with her ships; she must have seen with pride the discipline and devotion which have been shown to her and her Government by all her troops drawn from every part of her Empire. I leave it to the illustrious Duke [the Duke of Cambridge] in whose presence I speak, to bear witness to the Imperial patriotism which has been exhibited by the troops from India, which he recently reviewed at Malta. But it is not on our Fleets and Armies, however necessary they may be for the maintenance of Imperial strength, that I alone or mainly depend in that enterprize on which this country is about to enter. It is on what I most highly value — the consciousness that in the Eastern Nations there is a confidence in this country, and that, while we know we can enforce our policy, at the same time they know that our Empire is an Empire of liberty, of truth, and of justice. (3 *Hansard* 241: 1774)

At a Conservative banquet in Knightsbridge, Salisbury confirmed that the government was 'striving to pick up the thread — the broken thread — of England's old Imperial traditions'. The fusion of Britain's foreign policy and her imperial policy was complete.

It seemed that a new imperial age was being born. Gladstone, who was described at this time as like a caged tiger whose bone had been taken away, was white with rage. He penned a further sharp rebuke to the government in an article entitled 'England's Mission', in the *Nineteenth Century* for September 1878; this shifted the attack to the general principles guiding Disraeli's foreign and imperial policies. He began by denouncing the claim to have brought back 'peace with honour'. Where was the honour in allying with the oppressors of Christians, in occupying Cyprus, interfering in the Malay States and Egypt and annexing the Fiji Islands and the Transvaal? Disraeli's policy was one of 'territorial aggrandisement, backed by military display'. The British empire did not need Bosnian submissions — territories in which the British could only pose as masters. Where was the high moral purpose in this? He then took the battle to the enemy's own ground of empire. The Liberal view of empire was one of mutual advantage: of self-governing colonies of British stock freely associated, through ties of kindred and affection, with the mother country. This was a far nobler view than the alien idea which involved the expansion of British dominion over alien peoples, rule by force, overseas ventures and arbitrary actions which undermined the authority of Parliament and the British constitution.
[DOCUMENT XI]

The following month, Robert Lowe contributed a long philippic on 'Imperialism', and its impact on the domestic scene, to the *Fortnightly Review*. It was a powerful condemnation. **[DOCUMENT XII]** And in the Commons, Sir William Harcourt continued the attack in December 1878: the government 'had aroused a spirit which they could not repress; they had summoned this war spirit as their slave, and it had become their master . . . The policy of the government was an Imperial policy. Yes, it was an Imperial policy — it was a servile copy of the Imperialism of the Second Empire'.

'Imperialism' was having a bad press. Carnarvon, who left Disraeli's administration in January 1878, laboured in vain to stem the tide. In an address on 'Imperial Administration' at Edinburgh, he confessed: 'I have heard of Imperial policy, and Imperial interests, but Imperialism, as such, is a newly coined word to me.' He then went on to distinguish between a false imperialism — Caesarism, personal rule, continental despotism — and 'true' imperialism which was a service to mankind — maintaining peace, relieving famine, educating people, developing economies and generally serving the interests of others and so gaining the loyalty of millions of natives and British settlers alike. **[DOCUMENT XIII]**

An ideological battle over the two opposed views of empire now began. The economic depression of the winter of 1878–9 was the result, the Liberals asserted, of imperial wars and reckless expenditure. Unfortunately for Disraeli, 1879 witnessed setbacks in the Zulu and Afghan wars. At the Guildhall in November 1878, Disraeli exulted in Britain's imperial mission. He informed Lady Bradford, 'The party is what is called on its legs again, and jingoism triumphant!' A year later he was very much on the defensive: he knew the citizens of London were not ashamed of their empire, or the sentiment of patriotism, nor would they 'be beguiled into believing that in maintaining their Empire they may forfeit their liberties. One of the greatest of Romans, when asked what were his politics, replied, *Imperium et Libertas*. That would not make a bad programme for a British Ministry. It is one from which Her Majesty's advisers do not shrink.' Gladstone immediately retorted that Disraeli's empire and liberty meant 'Liberty for ourselves, Empire over the rest of mankind'.

In November 1879, believing that a dissolution of Parliament would soon be announced, Gladstone went north to his newly adopted constituency in Midlothian in a 'moral rage'. The final act was fought out before massed audiences in Scotland. In a carefully

planned series of set speeches, he unleashed his onslaught on
'Beaconsfieldism', concentrating on Disraeli's financial, imperial and
foreign policies: warmongering annexations and occupations, a
disregard for human life and individual liberties, reckless
expenditure, costly wars, the unashamed use of Indian troops, the
constant bypassing of Parliament, the wasting of British resources
and the stretching of British power beyond the limits of prudence.
Disraeli placed prestige above morality and revelled in 'military
sway' over alien peoples and the autocratic exercise of imperial
diplomacy. Nothing infuriated Gladstone more than the use of
Indian troops during the parliamentary recess in a renewed
campaign against Afghanistan. 'We have', he roared, 'gone up into
the mountains; we have broken Afghanistan to pieces; we have driven
mothers and children forth from their homes to perish in the snow;
we have spent treasure, of which a real account has never yet been
rendered; we have undergone an expenditure of which as yet I
believe we are aware of but a fraction.' True, India had to be
defended, but that did not mean Britain had a right to interfere
in every development affecting every avenue of approach to its
eastern possessions: 'That, gentlemen, is a monstrous claim.'
[DOCUMENT XIV]
The arrows hit their mark. Where crowds had cheered Disraeli on
his return from Berlin, audiences now warmed to the criticisms of
Gladstone following British reverses in Zululand and Afghanistan,
the increasing financial difficulties and rising taxes, and the
deepening agricultural and industrial depressions. In the election of
1880, accusations concerning 'imperialism' and 'Beaconsfieldism'
became millstones around Disraeli's neck. He may not have 'read a
single line' of this 'pilgrimage of passion', but the absence of any
effective reply from the Conservative front bench gave the
impression that none was possible. Gladstone certainly scored an
outstanding personal success at the hustings. In the ensuing general
election, the Liberals received a majority of over one hundred seats.
Once again, God had placed an ace up Gladstone's sleeve: 'the
Almighty has employed me for His purposes, in a manner larger, or
more especial than before, and has strengthened me and led me on
accordingly.'

Was Disraeli a romantic dreamer when it came to empire or did he
have a Machiavellian scheme to subvert the constitution and

promote personal rule? Disraeli certainly does not seem to have had any coherent plans. In part, the Conservatives were victims of their own propaganda. It was the flamboyance of Disraeli's imperialist rhetoric, his personality and ambitions, and what people thought he was capable of, that lay at the heart of their interpretation of events. On the other hand, there were authoritarian aspects to Disraeli's government. There was also a very clear difference between Gladstone and Disraeli in their attitudes and approaches to imperial matters. It was not simply a matter of presentation and style.

What contribution, then, did Disraeli make to the history of the British empire and the development of British imperialism? And what role did he play in the New Imperialism? In 1880, Gladstone marvelled at the sudden downfall of Beaconsfieldism and compared it to 'the vanishing of some vast magnificent castle in an Italian romance'. Subsequent events, however, suggest that Disraeli was far more in tune with his times than his slightly younger rival and that the legacy of his ideas, far from disappearing in 1880, survived well into the twentieth century.

6.   The Prophet of the New Imperialism?

In his election manifesto of March 1880, Beaconsfield attempted to play the 'peace and empire' cards for almost the last time by raising the spectre of Irish Home Rule:

> there are some who challenge the expediency of the imperial character of this realm . . . Having attempted, and failed, to enfeeble our colonies by their policy of decomposition, they may perhaps now recognise in the disintegration of the United Kingdom a mode which will not only accomplish but precipitate their purpose. (Monypenny and Buckle; op. cit., VI, 515)

In Europe, peace could not be maintained by the passive principle of non-intervention: 'Peace rests on the presence, not to say the ascendancy, of England in the councils of Europe.' Gladstone immediately described Beaconsfield's warnings as 'baseless' and 'terrifying insinuations' whose true purpose was 'to hide from view the acts of the ministry and their effect on the character and condition of the country'. He returned to his Midlothian campaign, attacking the extravagant waste and the reckless pursuit of 'phantoms of glory' that constituted 'Beaconsfieldism', and urged the nation to bring in a verdict of 'Guilty' in the great 'State Trial' that was about to take place. The voters, too concerned with their own hardships to worry about Ireland or Europe, let alone the empire, returned the verdict requested of them.

Beaconsfield, now aged seventy-five, met a group of 500 peers and MPs at Bridgewater House on 19 May 1880 and tried to raise their spirits. They should support the government against its own left wing, 'the party of revolution'. 'The policy of the Conservative party is to maintain the *Empire* and preserve the *Constitution*', he said. Had the result of the election been different he might have retired; as it was, 'in the hour of failure' he felt it his duty to continue as their leader. For once, his leadership was not contested and he was cheered to the rafters.

Beaconsfield was, however, becoming physically frail. He rose, having swallowed one drug and inhaled another, to make his last speech of any note in the Lords on 9 March 1881, protesting at the government's decision to give up Kandahar. He informed his peers: 'The key of India is London. The majesty and sovereignty, the spirit and vigour of your Parliament, the inexhaustible resources, the ingenuity and determination of your people — these are the keys of India.' Within a fortnight he was confined to his bed, apparently suffering from an attack of gout. It was soon apparent that he was declining fast. He died on 19 April 1881, before the age of the New Imperialism had visibly dawned.

How should Disraeli's imperial career be assessed? His record, as in most things, is certainly an unusual one. Despite all that has been written to the contrary about Disraeli's 'imperial consciousness', he undoubtedly possessed this in a very large measure — from his first political pamphlet when he spoke of 'the glory of the empire', to his last speeches in both the Commons and the Lords, by which time he had made empire one of the great planks of the Conservative party.

> Not insensible to the principle of progress, I have endeavoured to reconcile change with that respect for tradition which is one of the main elements of our social strength; and in external affairs I have endeavoured to develop and strengthen our Empire, believing that combination of achievement and responsibility elevates the character and condition of a people. (Letter to constituents, Hughenden Manor, 21 August 1876)

was the parting farewell to his constituents on the conferment of his earldom in 1876.

Such a long-term commitment was unusual, not only in one who, we are told, lacked any political principles whatsoever, but in a politician of this period. While those who had a continuous interest in empire usually concentrated on the colonies of British settlement and talked of creating 'so many happy Englands' overseas, Disraeli concentrated on the power, status and prestige conferred by empire in a way that not even Palmerston had done. Disraeli was a man of ideas who prided himself on his imaginative leadership. India and the Orient, which he had visited in his youth, fired his imagination. It was the grandeur and the romance of it all that captured him. He happily talked of colonists who found a gold nugget or fleeced a thousand flocks, and Indians who clamoured to pay homage to their empress-queen. Yet he was also the most hard-headed of statesmen, prepared to impose his will on native king, sultan, khedive and amir as and when necessary, and he did not blanch at bringing Indian troops to sort out the affairs of Europe. Nor was he always scrupulous in taking Parliament and even his own Cabinet colleagues into his confidence before undertaking a dramatic step. He delighted in creating an air of romance and mystery. It did not always redound to his credit and he was constantly misunderstood.

Disraeli did not possess any 'theory of empire'. It was the use that could be made of empire that interested him. Having set the tone and direction of policy, he left ministers to carry out the humdrum day-to-day administration of their departments. Except where foreign affairs and India were concerned, or when some coup was in the offing, he rarely interfered. He often offered encouragement and advice when asked; the Cabinet usually became involved only in matters of great import or at times of crisis. Consequently, ministers had a great deal of freedom and upsets occasionally ensued — such embarrassments as the mishandling of the Merchant Shipping Bill, the Fugitive Slave Circular and the proposed exchange of the Gambia.

It comes as no surprise to learn that Disraeli showed little interest in the details of colonial problems and had no interest in the formulation of policy towards the dependent empire, India excluded. So far as the self-governing colonies were concerned, he accepted the grant of responsible government but protested at the remaining anomalies, especially concerning defence, which involved the mother country in additional expenditure and commitments over which she had little control. He regretted that no attempt had been made to reconstruct the relationship: 'I think a great empire, founded on sound principles of freedom and equality, is as conducive to the spirit and power of a community as commercial prosperity or military force.' The self-governing colonies would 'in due time exercise their influence over the distribution of power' in the world. He looked forward to the day when these great colonies would be our allies.

For Disraeli, the empire was 'the visible expression of the power of England in the affairs of the world'. He was determined, therefore, that the advantages its possession conferred should not be whittled away by the 'Little England' ideas of so many Liberals. He protested at any proposed diminution of territory since it would indicate Britain's loss of authority and be a blow to her prestige. He constantly protested at the 'dogmas of political scientists and abstract enquirers' and the misguided views of 'prigs and pedants'. On the other hand, he was not an advocate of expansion; nor was he a supporter of imperial wars and he objected to the Ashanti, Perak, and Zulu wars. Many of his problems were due to ineffective oversight of ministers and insufficient control of men on the spot.

At least in Indian affairs Disraeli displayed a closer interest and took the lead in urging a more forward-looking policy. But the Royal Titles Act, which caused so many problems, and the Afghan war itself were not of Disraeli's creation. Nevertheless, two further elements were added to the indictment against 'Beaconsfieldism'. 'Remember', intoned Gladstone, 'that the sanctity of life in the hill villages of Afghanistan among the winter snows is as inviolable in the eye of Almighty God as can be your own.'

It was in the realm of foreign policy, however, that Gladstone claimed to detect the most dangerous aspects of Disraeli's imperial ideas. Just as Disraeli had little interest in the 'white man's burden' and the concept of England's civilizing mission (though he was quite prepared to mouth the sentiments when it was to his advantage to do so), so in foreign policy he had no time for small nations 'struggling to be free' or the internationalism preached by Gladstone. His was *realpolitik* without even 'a window-dressing of diplomatic morality'. Disraeli was not prepared to sacrifice 'national interests' to moral principles. But it was his words as much as his actions that alarmed opponents (as well as some supporters): the grandiose speeches which accompanied the purchase of the Suez Canal Company shares and the Royal Titles Bill; the histrionic performances following the brazen dispatch of Indian troops to Malta, the Anglo-Turkish military alliance and the occupation of Cyprus, all without resort to Parliament. A final straw was the use of Indian troops in the war against Afghanistan during a parliamentary recess. It was the cumulative impact of these words and deeds which, with the benefit of hindsight, made it possible for Disraeli's critics to see a malign strategy underlying the government's conduct of affairs.

That such grand strategy existed was manifestly untrue. Balfour recorded Salisbury's comments: Disraeli as a politician was 'exceedingly short sighted though very clear sighted. He neither would nor could look far ahead, or attempt to balance remote possibilities: though he rapidly detected the difficulties of the immediate situation and found the easiest if not the best solution for them'. With Disraeli at the head of affairs 'who *could* not look far a-head, and with a man like Derby at the Foreign Office who *would* not look far a-head, we naturally drifted'. Northcote, as leader of the Commons, complained that he could not explain the government's policy since he had no idea what it was: 'at present we seem to be living from hand to mouth, with no true conception of our own, or any other Power's policy'.

Nevertheless, the wars, annexations, and other isolated and unrelated aspects of the government's colonial and foreign policies, were interpreted by Disraeli's opponents as part of a hidden agenda to create a centralized military empire, to undermine Parliament, and to open the door to presidential or personal rule. Did not the creation of the Queen as Empress of India exalt the royal prerogative and graft an alien autocratic and military name and style onto the constitution? And was not the dispatch of Indian troops to Malta the action of men whose 'conception of the position, potency and functions of the British Empire is somewhat more exalted and more far-reaching than that of persons who are by instinct insular, and by habit parochial'? One observer feared there would soon be 'the whiff of grapeshot' at Westminster and Disraeli's old enemy, Robert Lowe, railed against a ministry which ruled by 'tricks, surprises, equivocations and concealment'. 'What we are disputing about', argued Gladstone, 'is a whole system of government.'

In many ways the government was a victim of its own propaganda. The flamboyance of Disraeli's gestures, his personality and ambitions, and what he was thought to be capable of, were at the back of the minds of many critics. His imperial rhetoric confirmed their fears. And their suspicions were not entirely without foundation. Such rhetoric did encourage subordinates in aggressive actions and defiant acts in the belief that while they might be exceeding their instructions, they were acting within the spirit of Disraelian imperialism. It provided the ideological fuel. The critics were also correct in detecting an authoritarian aspect to Disraeli's policies. Parliament was knowingly bypassed on occasion. Cabinet meetings were not held because there was 'nothing to discuss'. Policy was often hammered out by Disraeli, Derby and Salisbury behind the scenes, in much the same way as Disraeli had previously settled matters in sole consultation with Derby's father. A message was even sent to the Tsar, at the height of the Eastern Question crisis, claiming quite untruthfully that the Cabinet was united on military intervention if Russia opened a new campaign.

Disraeli was convinced that if Britain wished to resume her place in the 'natural order' as a great power, she must act as one. Highly conscious of the changed world situation after 1870, with the re-emergence of the United States from its civil war, the rise of Prussia and the new German empire in Europe, French expansion in Cochin China, Russian advances in central Asia, the Balkans and Asia Minor, and the Westernization of Japan, he wished to use the empire as a counterbalance in the struggle for ascendancy. He did not hesitate to use the resources at his disposal, especially the military might of the Indian army manned and paid for by the Indians themselves. It was this coming together of Disraeli's interests in India and the East, and his suspicion of Russia, together with the denunciations of his opponents, that gave him the reputation of being a pioneer and prophet of the New Imperialism.

What did Disraeli add to the character of British imperialism? It is usually asserted that Disraeli's major contributions came in the form of an outburst of jingoism (which was a facet of British life especially prominent during the closing years of the nineteenth century), and the linking of patriotism with the Conservative party. During the heightened passions of 1877–8, contemporaries remarked on the alliance of Toryism and rowdyism which Gladstone described as 'a stirring of all the foul dregs of the coarsest and rankest material among us'. While Disraeli noted the mood, it is doubtful whether the movement was either of his making or to his taste. Salisbury reported from Berlin that Beaconsfield was 'much disgusted at the Jingo outbreak in England' and the 'extravagant nonsense' talked about the Russian acquisition of Batum. Salisbury put it down to the 'silly season' and the 'hot weather'. It should also be remembered that there was an equally popular alternative to the 'By Jingo!' song that was often sung on the same music hall bill:

> I don't want to fight, I'll be slaughtered if I do!
> I'll change my togs and sell my kit and pop my rifle too!
> I don't like the war, I ain't no Briton true,
> And I'll let the Russians have Constantinople.

In any case, the jingoism of 1877–8 was a very short-lived affair and was of no use to the Conservatives in the election of 1880. One noteworthy outcome, however, was the decision of Ellis Ashmead Bartlett, who helped to organize the break-up of the Hyde Park peace demonstrations, to found a 'Patriotic Association' for the 'defence of the honour and interests of England, and the maintenance intact of the British Empire'. In March 1880, Bartlett launched a new journal, *England*, a penny weekly aimed at the working and lower middle classes. Disraeli rewarded him with a 'pocket borough' in the 1880 election.

The harnessing of patriotism to the Conservative party had been a long-term aim of Disraeli. This was behind his persistent attempts to brand the Liberals as the 'cosmopolitan' party and the Tories as the 'national' party. The basic issue, as Disraeli put it at the Crystal Palace, was whether England should be 'modelled and moulded upon Continental principles and in due course meet an inevitable fate', or whether it should be 'an imperial country, a country where your sons when they rise, rise to paramount positions, and obtain, not merely the esteem of your countrymen but command the respect of the world'.

It was an attempt to reassure middle-class supporters and attract new working-class voters. It helped to transform the liberal nationalism of mid-century into the more aggressive, conservative nationalism of the late nineteenth century. Hugh Cunningham has suggested that 'the decisive shift came suddenly in the space of a few months in late 1877 and early 1878', during the Eastern Question crisis. Certainly by 1880, the Conservatives were firmly associated with the empire and Disraeli's followers were regularly called 'imperialists'. Disraeli's rhetoric had played its part, but so had Gladstone's invective. The increasingly bitter rivalry between the two men caused their positions to be polarized — and the Bulgarian atrocities proved an agonizing case for the future Liberal Imperialists. On 11 March 1880, *The Times* noted:

> 'Imperialism' was a word invented to stamp Lord Beaconsfield's supposed designs with popular reprobation. But the weapon wounded the hand that wielded it, and a suspicion was engendered, which seriously injured the Liberal cause, that Liberalism was in some sort an antithesis of Imperialism. It will cost Lord Hartington and his associates not a little pain to eradicate this popular belief.

Empire had been hijacked by the Conservative party.

Was Disraeli, with his highly publicized concept of a centralized empire, acting in support of Great Britain on the world's stage and openly glorying in a military sway over distant peoples, the prophet of the New Imperialism? Clearly a new imperialism was in the making, but whether Disraeli's 'bombastic school' ('lost in wonder and ecstasy' at the empire's immense dimensions, as Seeley put it) was of the same ilk as the belligerent, expanding New Imperialism of the coming decades must remain open to doubt.

Disraeli had never preached imperial expansion except where British strategic interests necessitated the taking of some 'strong place' in the world. True, some expansion did occur during his second ministry, but this was the result of crises on the imperial frontier or Carnarvon's own personal designs. Claims to paramountcy had been the normal response. But by the end of the decade, times were changing as the whole fabric of empire became more brittle. Carnarvon began to talk of a sort of Monroe Doctrine in the South Pacific. And in Africa,

> I should not like anyone to come too near us either on the South towards the Transvaal, which *must* be ours; or on the north too near to Egypt and the country which belongs to Egypt. In fact when I speak of geographical limits I am not expressing my real opinion. We cannot admit rivals in the East or even the central parts of Africa. (C. C. Eldridge, *England's Mission: The Imperial Idea in the Age of Gladstone and Disraeli, 1868–80* (London, Macmillan, 1973), 245–6)

Even Lord Derby admitted that New Guinea might have to be annexed and Disraeli, Salisbury and Northcote agreed that if Russia became a Mediterranean power, 'we seem bound by the law of self-preservation to assure ourselves of Egypt'. Further afield, Salisbury advised Cranbrook: 'I think you will have to take Burmah. As a matter of political convenience I should prefer to postpone it till after the general election: but I doubt whether you will have the choice.'

All these opinions were reactions to events, rather than part of any Conservative philosophy of empire. Even in 1880 there was no expansionist fervour. Disraeli never showed much interest in Africa, apart from Egypt. No doubt many of his actions and much of his rhetoric created an atmosphere in which interest in empire and talk of expansion could flourish, but it took political and economic changes in Europe in the 1880s, the collapse of indigenous regimes like that of the khedive in Egypt, and the burgeoning interest of European rivals in the acquisition of colonies, to spark off the scrambles for territory and concessions in Africa, central Asia, the Pacific, south-east Asia and the Far East.

After Gladstone's mid-Victorian recipe of free trade, the concert of Europe, informal rule, non-intervention and minimum responsibility had failed miserably in solving the problems Britain faced in a world of jealous and competing nations, Disraeli's name began to acquire a new glamour. People remembered his striking imperial rhetoric, the Crystal Palace address, the strong assertion of British interests, and his awakening of the imperial spirit. Disraeli's creation as a prophet of the New Imperialism was very much the product of a later generation. In 1898, J. Holland Rose, in his *Rise and Growth of Democracy in Great Britain*, wrote of his 'prescience as to the broader issues of imperialism . . . However much the imperialism of Lord Beaconsfield may be criticised in regard to details, there can be little doubt now that he laid down the general lines of policy which must be followed by the British race, if it is to hold a foremost place in the world'. In 1921, a reviewer of Buckle's final volume of the *Life of Benjamin Disraeli* could write that Disraeli had 'formulated the theory of Empire, which, rejected for a time by Gladstone, gradually became the accepted ideal not only of Great Britain herself, but of the British Dominions and the Empire as a whole'. It was pure myth.

Is this yet another example of the Disraeli legend at work? Disraeli did contribute something lasting to the character of British imperialism. Perhaps it needed the 'foreign' Disraeli to inject a foreign ingredient into the hitherto colourless character of British imperial sentiment: an unashamed, militant, illiberal and undemocratic spirit glorying in the achievements of British rule overseas. It was a facet of British imperialism which remained characteristic of the British national outlook until well into the twentieth century (and can still surface in moments of national tension and excitement, such as the Suez crisis in 1956, the Falklands war of 1982 and the more recent Gulf war). The Falklands war, in particular, was like a rerun of one of Queen Victoria's 'little wars' and there were many reminders of Disraeli. The very first of these highly publicized wars overseas that became a newspaper event was the Abyssinian campaign during Disraeli's first administration. The activities and reporting of the 'gutter press' during the Falklands war were not only reminiscent of the 'yellow press' during the Boer war, but date back to the first outburst of 'jingoism' in 1877–8.

The association of empire with the Conservative party dates from the time of Disraeli, and the division into the two schools of imperialist thought represented by Gladstone and Disraeli dominated British policy for the next fifty years. Fundamental questions about 'the character of the state and the exercise of its power at home and abroad' were raised and continued to be debated throughout the life of the empire. Disraeli's contribution was the concept of 'a powerful

England, strengthened by the resources and peoples of a far-flung empire, playing a decisive role in world affairs'. In an age of large empires, the idea of a compact, centralized empire, commanded from the centre, its collective forces ready for instant combat, had far more appeal than the Gladstonian concept of a loosely knit association of self-governing states. It was a role surrendered with great reluctance in the years following the Second World War.

Disraeli preached power, status and prestige from before he entered Parliament until his death. From 1833 to 1881, he reminded the electors constantly of the greatness and glory of empire. Koebner and Schmidt have concluded that he gave the empire 'a new ring of power and confident assertion'. This is not to deny that his interest was selective, that he was an opportunist at times, and that he sometimes used empire for domestic purposes. There does, however, seem to be a consistency about this aspect of Disraeli's career which many historians, if not most, have found lacking elsewhere.

Should Disraeli's sincerity be doubted? Was the difference between Gladstone and Disraeli really nothing more than a matter of rhetoric, presentation and style, as recent historians such as P. R. Ghosh, John Walton and Ian Machin have suggested? Surely, in the field of empire the differences were too great. Gladstone always spoke of the burdens and responsibilities of empire, of moral obligations, duty and sacrifice: Disraeli concentrated on power, prestige, 'national interest', military and commercial advantage. Would Gladstone ever have declared about an imperial war: 'money is not to be considered in such matters: success alone is to be thought of'? More to the point, would Gladstone have purchased the Suez Canal Company shares, made Queen Victoria Empress of India, sent Indian troops to Malta and occupied Cyprus?

None the less, arguments will doubtless continue to rage about Disraeli's consistency, his principles, his sincerity, his rhetoric, ideas, slogans and presentation. He loved romance and mystery. When he died, a colleague, though hardly a friend, acutely observed:

> It is the close of a strange and most remarkable career, the strangest of any of our time in England, and I doubt much if there is any one living who combines all the conditions for a faithful description and analysis of so singular a life and character. It is most probable I think that he will go down to posterity a curious theme of speculation and controversy — such in a great measure as he has been during his life. (Hardinge, op. cit., II, 62–3)

The speculation and the controversy still continue.

Illustrative Documents

DOCUMENT I The Letters of Runnymede: Lord Glenelg, 12 March 1836

While seeking election to Parliament, Disraeli wrote a series of open letters to The Times, *under the pseudonym of 'Runnymede', addressed to some of the leading politicians of the day. Letter XIII lampoons the colonial secretary, Lord Glenelg.*

MY LORD, — Let me not disturb your slumbers too rudely: I will address you in a whisper, and on tiptoe. At length I have succeeded in penetrating the recesses of your enchanted abode. The knight who roused the Sleeping Beauty could not have witnessed stranger marvels in his progress than he who has at last contrived to obtain an interview with the sleeping Secretary.

The moment that I had passed the Foreign Office an air of profound repose seemed to pervade Downing Street, and as I approached the portal of your department, it was with difficulty I could resist the narcotic influence of the atmosphere . . . I found your clerks yawning, and your under-secretaries just waking from a dream. A dozy, drowsy, drony hum, the faint rustling of some papers like the leaves of autumn, and a few noiseless apparitions gliding like ghosts, just assured me that the business of the nation was not neglected. Every personage and every incident gradually prepared me for the quiescent presence of the master mind, until, adroitly stepping over your private secretary, nodding and recumbent at your threshold, I found myself before your Lordship, the guardian of our colonial empire, stretched on an easy couch in luxurious listlessness, with all the prim voluptuousness of a puritanical Sardanapalus.[1]

I forget who was the wild theorist who enunciated the absurd doctrine that 'ships, colonies, and commerce' were the surest foundations of the empire. What an infinitely ridiculous idea! But the march of intellect and the spirit of the age have cleansed our brains of this perilous stuff. Had it not been for the invention of ships, the great malady of sea-sickness, so distressing to an indolent Minister, would be unknown; colonies, like country-houses, we have long recognised to be sources only of continual expense, and to be kept up merely from a puerile love of show; as for commerce, it is a vulgarism, and fit only for low people ...

Affairs, . . . my dear Lord Glenelg, are far from disheartening, especially in that department under your own circumspect supervision. What if the Mauritius be restive — let the inhabitants cut each others' throats: that will ultimately produce peace. What if Jamaica be in flames — we still have East India sugar; and by the time we have lost that, the manufacture of beetroot will be perfect. What if Colonel Torrens,[2] perched on the . . . height of a joint-stock company, be transporting our fellow-countrymen to the milk and honey of Australia, without even the preparatory ceremony of a trial by jury — let the exiles settle this great constitutional question with the kangaroos. What if Canada be in rebellion — let not the menacing spectre of Papineau[3] or the suppliant shade of the liberal Gosford[4] scare your Lordship's dreams. Slumber on without a pang, most vigilant of Secretaries. I will stuff you a fresh pillow with your unanswered letters, and insure you a certain lullaby by reading to you one of your own despatches.

(W. Hutcheon (ed.), *Whigs and Whiggism: Political Writings by Benjamin Disraeli* (London, 1913), 297–301.)

1. King of Assyria, subject of a poetic drama by Lord Byron in 1821.
2. Robert Torrens, political economist.
3. Louis-Joseph Papineau, rebel leader in Lower Canada.
4. Earl of Gosford, Governor of Lower Canada.

DOCUMENT II   Disraeli's 'Old England' letters to *The Times*, 11 January 1838 and 13 January 1838

In the wake of the Canadian rebellions, Disraeli wrote another series of letters to The Times, *many in the literary style of Thomas Carlyle, accusing the Whigs of stripping the government of moral power. The Duke of Wellington's question in 1831 — 'How is the King's Government to be carried on?' — had yet to be answered.*

Crisis has spoken out; his conversation with John Bull yesterday was frank. This visitor, whom all talk of, many fear, has told John Bull the truth. He has at length come to our shores. He had given us seven years to answer the Duke's great question — 'How is the King's Government to be carried on?' We have not answered it, and now Crisis has arrived. Was it not time? Colonies revolting without practical grievances and without power or capability of independence; plainly because they were not governed; colonies revolting, not because they were misgoverned or could govern themselves, but because they were not governed at all. It is time for Crisis to appear.

Is Canada the only portion of the realm that is not governed? — that rebels, in short, because it is not controlled? Are there any others? Why has the power of government of the British Empire in so many quarters degenerated into mere administration? As a nation, are we less brave, less rich, less powerful, than heretofore? We have fleets and armies; we have a great revenue. Why, in the words of the great Duke — why, then, cannot the government be carried on, when all visible means of government are at hand? It must be answered; it cannot longer be delayed. The whole nation cries out: 'Question, question.'

★　　★　　★

In every part of the kingdom and the empire, authority has dwindled into a mere affair of administration. Government has lost its moral power; it has degenerated into a mere formula, obeyed in Britain from habit and the love of order peculiar to the nation, the necessary quality of a people devoted to industry; obeyed in all other places according to circumstances, and of these the principal is, whether there be a sufficient physical force to uphold it. As long as there be a sufficient force, agitation only; if not a sufficient force, then revolt . . .

A powerful peerage, a powerful Church, a powerful gentry, a powerful colonial system, involving the interests of the merchant, the manufacturer, and the ship-owner, a powerful military system, a learned bar, a literary press — these were formerly some of the great interests on whose support the moral power of a British Government was founded. During the last seven years we have seen every one of these great interests attacked. And by whom? By the Ministers of the Crown.

They have denounced the peerage; they have attempted to

degrade the Church; they have held up the gentlemen of England to
public reprobation as bigoted oppressors; they have maintained
themselves in power by means of a party who have declared the
dominion of the metropolis over her colonies to be baneful;
they have disbanded the militia; they have menaced the bar; and they
have vainly attempted to annihilate the intelligence of the press. They
have themselves set an example to the mob to attack everything that
is established.

Can they be surprised that they themselves are at last attacked? . . .
Threatened themselves they exercise their formal power, and it fails
and must fail. What resource remains? None for the Whigs. They
cannot call for the support of those institutions and classes whom
they have taught the mob to hate and despise — the institutions and
classes that formed the empire, and by whom alone the empire can
be maintained. The Whigs have destroyed the moral influence of
Government.

(W. Hutcheon (ed.), *Whigs and Whiggism: Political Writings by Benjamin
Disraeli* (London, 1913), 426–8.)

DOCUMENT III   Disraeli's speech on the Indian Mutiny, delivered in the House of Commons on 27 July 1857

*In a long speech, Disraeli gave one of the earliest analyses of the causes of
the Indian Mutiny, blaming the policies of previous governments.*

Now, I apprehend that it is of the greatest importance to obtain as
clear an idea as we can of the causes which have led to these events
. . . It was alleged that, this being a mere military mutiny, all we had
to do was to put it down, and when it was put down, then the
Government would consider the condition of the Indian army. Now,
I humbly think that the question whether it is a mere military mutiny
is one of prime importance. Is it a military mutiny, or is it a national
revolt? Is the conduct of the troops the consequence of a sudden
impulse, or is it the result of an organized conspiracy? The House
must feel that, upon the right appreciation of that issue, the greatest
of all questions, namely, the measures which the Government ought
to adopt, or Parliament ought to sanction, entirely depends . . . I
shall show, or endeavour to show to the House to-night that our
Government in India of late years has alienated or alarmed almost

every influential class in the country. I shall show, or endeavour to show, to the House to-night that the mutual suspicions and prejudices between rival religions and different races, which were the cause of segregation between powerful classes in that country, have of late years, in consequence of our policy, gradually disappeared, and that for them has been substituted an identity of sentiments, and those sentiments, I am sorry to say, hostile to our authority . . .

. . . Of late years a great change has taken place in the Government of India. In olden days, and for a considerable time — indeed, until, I would say, the last ten years — the principle of our government of India, if I may venture to describe it in a sentence, was to respect Nationality . . . It will be found in that wonderful progress of human events which the formation of our Indian empire presents that our occupation of any country has been preceded by a solemn proclamation and concluded by a sacred treaty, in which we undertook to respect and maintain inviolate the rights and privileges, the laws and customs, the property and religion of the people, whose affairs we were about to administer. Such was the principle on which our Indian empire was founded; and it is a proud as well as a politic passage in the history of Englishmen, that principle has been until late years religiously observed . . . But, Sir, of late years a new principle appears to have been adopted in the government of India . . . Everything in India has been changed. Laws and manners, customs and usages, political organizations, the tenure of property, the religion of the people — everything in India has either been changed or attempted to be changed, or there is a suspicion among the population that a desire for change exists on the part of our Government. Now, taking the last ten years, I would range under three heads the various causes which have led, in my opinion, to a general discontent among all classes of that country with our rule. I would describe them thus — first, our forcible destruction of native authority; next, our disturbance of the settlement of property; and thirdly, our tampering with the religion of the people, I believe that directly or indirectly, all the principal causes of popular discontent or popular disturbance will range under those three heads . . .

Now, Sir, I will first address myself to the forcible destruction of native authority in the East by our Government, and in this subject are involved some of the most important principles of Indian policy. The House must recollect that even at the present time there are at least 200 Native Indian princes; they still govern a population of at least 60,000,000 of inhabitants. With all these princes the English

Government has treaties. These treaties differ in many particulars . . . but there is one feature of similarity throughout all these treaties — that is, an engagement on the part of the English Government with each Indian prince, that so long as the latter shall observe the conditions of the treaty, the English Government will secure to him and to his heirs for ever the throne upon which he sits. Now, Sir, about the year 1848 is what I fix as the date of the inauguration of the new system of Indian policy, which I shall show to be opposed to all the principles by which our empire was gained and established . . . About this time accordingly appeared one of the most important State papers that ever was published relating to India: it was a Minute of Council referring to the decease of an Indian prince, and in which was laid down the principle, almost without disguise, that the future Indian policy would be, to increase the revenue of our dominions by increasing our dominions themselves; that, in short, the only mode by which an enlarged revenue could be obtained was, by enlarging our territories . . . The Rajah of Sattara, as I have already reminded the House, died without natural heirs, but the House must also remember that the Hindoo system is such, that a family can never become extinct . . . The Governor General of India, however, in pursuance of the vigorous and novel policy which he had determined to establish in India, took the decided step of abolishing the law of adoption; he did not recognize the individual who had been proclaimed to all India as the son and successor of the deceased prince: but, claiming the equivocal right of suzerainty, or Lord Paramount, he ordered his troops to enter the Raj, and the Rajah of Sattara was absorbed into the dominions of the East India Company . . . Remember, the principle of the law of adoption is not solely the prerogative of princes and principalities in India; it applies to every man in Hindostan who has landed property and who professes the Hindoo religion . . . What man was safe? What feudatory, what freeholder who had not a child of his own loins was safe throughout India? These were not idle fears; they were extensively acted upon and reduced to practice . . . Here was a new source of revenue. But while all these things were acting upon the minds of these classes of Hindoos, the Government took another step to disturb the settlement of property . . .

The House is aware . . . that there are great portions of the land of India which are free from land-tax . . . The origin of the grants under which these lands are held is difficult to penetrate, but some are undoubtedly of great antiquity . . . Commissions were issued to inquire into titles to landed estates in the Presidency of Bengal and adjoining territory . . . I am induced to believe the amount obtained by the Government of India in this manner — that is, by the resumption of estates from their proprietors — is not less in the Presidency of Bengal alone than £500,000 a year. Conceive what a capital is represented by such an annual revenue! Conceive the thousands and tens of thousands of estates that must have been resumed by the Government from the proprietors to obtain such a result! . . . But there is another source of revenue, which during the last few years recourse has been had to, and with respect to which the results, as regards the opinions and sentiments of the population, are not less important. The House will understand that when we gradually obtained absolute predominance over the great kingdoms of India we often left a nominal authority — the pomp and pageant of power — to the Native Princes, to whom and to their heirs and chief dependents, the Government accorded pensions. They were perpetual pensions . . . Now, under the new system these pensions have been discontinued, and are to be considered as annuities only. The House will see that this conversion of hereditary pensions into personal annuities is confiscation by a new means, but on a most extensive, startling, and shocking scale, because the descendants of those ancient Royal Families and nobles find themselves by this new rule reduced to a state of the utmost humiliation, and the people see their ancient Sovereigns, whose deposition from political power they might for many reasons feel a loss, reduced to almost absolute beggary . . . The House will see, therefore, with reference to the second point, how far the Government have disturbed the settlement of property, by their conduct with regard to the resumption of lands, by abolishing the principle of adoption, and by changing into annuities those pensions on condition of paying which we became lords of the sovereignties. That, then, I say, is the second great cause which has produced general discontent throughout India, and has estranged numerous and powerful classes from that authority which I think on the whole they were disposed to regard with deference.

Sir, I have now to approach the third point — that of tampering with the religion of the people of India. This, I am aware, is one of those subjects which are called difficult and delicate; but, in my opinion, no subject is difficult or delicate when the existence of an empire is at stake, and I shall therefore address myself to this point without any undue reserve . . . So far from the Hindoo looking with suspicion upon the missionaries, I am convinced, from what I have read and heard, that the Hindoo is at all times ready to discuss theological questions with the missionary . . . But what the Hindoo does dread — what he regards with the utmost jealousy — what he looks upon with undying apprehension — is the union of missionary enterprise with the political power of the Government . . . No taxation however grievous, no injustice however glaring, acts so dangerously on the Hindoo character as the persuasion that the authority of the Crown is exercised to induce him to abandon the religion of his forefathers. Now, have the Government of India lent a sanction to the suspicion of the Hindoos? . . . I must say, after examining the subject, I am sure with impartiality, that it appears to me that the Legislative Council of India have, under the new system, been constantly nibbling at the religious system of the natives . . . I do not say that in establishing a national system of education for the Hindoos you have gone ostentatiously into their schools with the Sacred Scriptures; but I am very much misinformed if the Sacred Scriptures have not suddenly appeared in those schools; and you cannot persuade the Hindoos that they have appeared there without the concurrence or the secret sanction of the Government . . . There were, however, other acts on the part of the Government, which I regard as much more reprehensible, and which, as I shall show, have produced very evil consequences . . . The first was the law which enacted that no man should be deprived of his inheritance on account of a change of religion. That has occasioned great alarm in India. The House must understand that property is inherited in India by men as trustees for sacred purposes, and if a man does not lose his property who has changed his religion some of the principal ends and duties of that inheritance cannot be fulfilled. That is a change in the law which has created much alarm and suspicion. But there is also another law, which has, if possible, more alarmed the feelings of the Hindoos, and that is, the permission to a Hindoo widow to marry a second husband. What could have induced the Governor General of India to pass such a law it is, at this moment, difficult to conceive . . . These two laws have to my mind, more than any other cause, disquieted the religious feelings of the Hindoos, and prepared their minds for recent lamentable events . . .

It was under these circumstances . . . that an event occurred in India to the consequences of which I am now going to solicit your attention for a few moments. And that is the annexation of Oude, the effect of which, as I shall show, was of a peculiar and, as regards public opinion, if I may use the expression, of a generalizing character . . . The moment that the throne of Oude, occupied by its King, was declared vacant, and English troops were poured into his territory, the Mahomedan princes understood what would be their future fate. You see how the plot thickens. You have the whole of the Indian princes — men of different races and different religions — men between whom there were traditionary feuds and long and enduring prejudices, with all the elements to produce segregation — become united — Hindoos, Mahrattas, Mahomedans — secretly feeling a common interest and a common cause. Not only the princes but the proprietors are against you . . . But the annexation of Oude brought more than all this. Although you had alienated from you the hearts of princes and proprietors — although you had poisoned the former affection and veneration of the peasantry — there was a class in India which, if you had allowed it to remain faithful, might have enabled even the new system to have triumphed. It turned out that the great proportion of the Bengal army were subjects of the King of Oude. I have been told . . . that there were not less than 70,000 men from Oude in our Indian armies and contingents . . . The Oude Sepoy returns now to his village, and finds it belongs to the Company, and that the rigid revenue system of India is applied to his small property . . . He finds he has lost political privileges and his territorial position; and for the first time, the great body of the Bengal army is disaffected. How does that act? With the princes, the proprietors, and the religious classes, all for a long time distrustful and disaffected: the opportunity occurs, and the only class which can keep them in order is angry and discontented . . . The annexation of Oude took place in 1856. This is only the middle of 1857 . . .

. . . I think I have said enough to induce the House to pause before they form too precipitate an opinion upon the causes of the disasters in India. I think I have said enough to make the House at least feel that it is not by saying that we have to deal with a mere mutiny that we shall save India. But, I said, and I think I have shown, that the condition of things was this — that the people of India were only waiting for an occasion and a pretext. That occasion was soon furnished, and that pretext was soon devised.

(*Hansard's Parliamentary Debates,* Third series, vol. 147, cols. 440–72
passim.)

DOCUMENT IV   Disraeli's speech on the defence of Canada, delivered in the House of Commons on 25 July 1862

After the Canadians failed to pass a Militia Bill to provide for their own defence, Disraeli comments on the relationship with the self-governing colonies.

Sir, I cannot contemplate with the same feeling of indifference as the Secretary of State a separation taking place between this country and Canada. I think a great empire, founded on sound principles of freedom and equality, is as conducive to the spirit and power of a community as commercial prosperity or military force; and therefore I should be very sorry under the present circumstances, after all that has occurred, to suppose that the connection between the mother country and this important colony should end. The resources of Canada are great and various. It has had the advantage of having been colonized during centuries by two of the most distinguished nations of Europe. Canada is, in fact, a reflex of those two powerful races, differing in their manners and even in their religious opinions; and therefore has many of these diverse elements which tend to change in due season a mere colonial into a national character. I do not think that the importance of Canada can be overstated, but, unfortunately, we feel every day more and more that the relations between the mother country and those colonies in which what we call self-government has been established are not altogether of a satisfactory nature. That self-government was for a long time so obstinately refused by the mother country, and in the end so precipitously conceded, that I will not say the terms, but the principles on which the new relations between the mother country and the colonies should hereafter be regulated were never sufficiently examined and matured. There were two principles on which the new connection might have been established, and which could not have been contested at the time when that self-government was formed and sanctioned. One was that every colony should adopt reasonable measures of self-defence; and the other that there should be between the colony and the mother country free commercial intercourse. I do not believe that at the time either of those principles would have been controverted, or refused by any colonies belonging to the English Crown, and now enjoying the blessings of self-government. It is impossible to deny that the heedlessness with which this great boon was conceded by England has brought about a very unsatisfactory state of relations between this country and those colonies to which self-government was granted; and this is especially remarkable in the case of Canada, from its great and preponderating importance; but I do not very well perceive how we can suddenly and hastily adopt a remedy for these evils. They are, in a great degree, the creation of our rashness and carelessness, and we must trust in the case of Canada, as well as in the case of other colonies similarly situated, to the spirit and sense of the inhabitants, and in a great degree to the character, talents, and resources of the governors whom we send out . . .

. . . For my own part I am anxious to maintain our colonial empire; but that I feel can be done only on principles of freedom and equality. If in olden days that empire was endangered because of a sense of oppression on the part of the colonists, it will in our day also be endangered if, on the part of the mother country, a sense of unfairness with regard to her connection with her dependencies should prevail. We ought not, however, to use the word 'dependencies' any longer. We should look upon those communities as a portion of a great empire in whose prosperity and honour we are alike interested. In that view of the case I look upon the colonial empire of England as being eminently conducive to her strength. The amount of the advantage which she derives from it cannot be measured by pounds, shillings, and pence, by commercial profits, or even by the military force with which at the moment of emergency our colonial connection might furnish us. I feel persuaded that the very fact that we belong to a great empire founded upon those principles of freedom and equality which are necessary for the prosperity of such an empire, is in itself a source of strength to England, from the elevation which it gives to the character of our fellow-subjects; while it influences the councils of Europe and the course of human events. Nor do I despair that the unsatisfactory state of things prevailing in Canada at the present moment, so far as relations between her and the mother country are concerned, will be modified and improved before long . . . I would simply repeat that I think the present disagreeable state of affairs in Canada has been mainly occasioned by the sending out there of 3,000 troops in the month of June in last year — a measure which at the time I deprecated; while I would express a hope that affairs in the colony may soon wear a more satisfactory aspect.

(*Hansard's Parliamentary Debates,* Third series, vol. 168, cols. 867–8, 871–2.)

DOCUMENT V Disraeli's letter to the earl of Malmesbury, 13 August 1852

In a letter to the foreign secretary, Disraeli makes a passing reference to the dispute with the United States concerning the Newfoundland fishing grounds.

... This Fisheries affair is a bad business. Pakington's circular is not written with a thorough knowledge of the circumstances. He is out of his depth, more than three marine miles from shore.

These wretched Colonies will all be independent, too, in a few years, and are a millstone round our necks. If I were you, I would *push matters* with Fillmore, who has no interest to pander to the populace like Webster, and make an honourable and speedy settlement.

(W. F. Monypenny and G. E. Buckle, *The Life of Benjamin Disraeli, Earl of Beaconsfield* (6 vols., London, 1910–20), vol.III, 385.)

DOCUMENT VI Disraeli's letter to the earl of Derby, 30 September 1866

After the hurried dispatch of troops to Canada, Disraeli writes to the prime minister about the problems involved in continuing to carry the main responsibility for the defence of Canada.

... Until the American elections have taken place, there will be no chance of anything like sense or moderation in American politics; but there will be a chance then.

Then, also, we must seriously consider our Canadian position, which is most illegitimate. An army maintained in a country which does not permit us even to govern it! What an anomaly!

It can never be our pretence, or our policy, to defend the Canadian frontier against the U.S. If the colonists can't, as a general rule, defend themselves against the Fenians, they can do nothing. They ought to be, and must be, strong enough for that. Power and influence we should exercise in Asia; consequently in Eastern Europe, consequently also in Western Europe; but what is the use of these colonial deadweights which *we do not govern*?

I don't regret what we did the other day about Canada, because the circumstances were very peculiar. A successful raid of the

Fenians was not off the cards, which would have upset your untried Ministry, and might have produced an insurrection in Ireland; and it was not fair to the Canadians, when, at last, they were making some attempts at self-defence, to allow them to be crushed in the bud of their patriotism. But the moment the American elections are over, we should withdraw the great body of our troops, and foster a complete development of self-government.

Leave the Canadians to defend themselves; recall the African squadron; give up the settlements on the west coast of Africa; and we shall make a saving which will, at the same time, enable us to build ships and have a good Budget.

What is more, we shall have accomplished something definite, tangible, for the good of the country. In these days more than ever, the people look to results. What we have done about Canada is perfectly defensible, if it is not looked upon as a permanent increase of our Canadian establishments.

(W. F. Monypenny and G. E. Buckle, *The Life of Benjamin Disraeli, Earl of Beaconsfield* (6 vols., London, 1910–20), vol.IV, 476–7.)

DOCUMENT VII Disraeli's speech at the Crystal Palace, 24 June 1872

Disraeli sets out the three great objectives of the Conservative party, the second of which is to uphold the empire.

Gentlemen, there is another and second great object of the Tory party. If the first is to maintain the institutions of the country, the second is, in my opinion, to uphold the Empire of England. If you look to the history of this country since the advent of Liberalism — forty years ago — you will find there has been no effort so continuous, so subtle, supported by so much energy, and carried on with so much ability and acumen, as the attempts of Liberalism to effect the disintegration of the Empire of England.

And, gentlemen, of all its efforts, this is the one which has been nearest to success. Statesmen of the highest character, writers of the most distinguished ability, the most organised and efficient means, have been employed in this endeavour. It has been proved to all of us that we have lost money by our colonies. It has been shown with precise, with mathematical demonstration, that there never was a jewel in the Crown of England that was so truly costly as the possession of India. How often has it been suggested that we should at once emancipate ourselves from this incubus. Well, that result was nearly accomplished. When those subtle views were adopted by the country under the plausible plea of granting self-government to the Colonies, I confess that I myself thought that the tie was broken. Not that I for one object to self-government. I cannot conceive how our distant colonies can have their affairs administered except by self-government. But self-government, in my opinion, when it was conceded, ought to have been conceded as part of a great policy of Imperial consolidation. It ought to have been accompanied by an Imperial tariff, by securities for the people of England for the enjoyment of the unappropriated lands which belonged to the Sovereign as their trustee, and by a military code which should have precisely defined the means and the responsibilities by which the colonies should be defended, and by which, if necessary, this country should call for aid from the colonies themselves. It ought, further, to have been accompanied by the institution of some representative council in the metropolis, which would have brought the Colonies into constant and continuous relations with the Home Government. All this, however, was omitted because those who advised that policy — and I believe that their convictions were sincere — looked upon the Colonies of England, looked even upon our connection with India, as a burden upon this country, viewing everything in a financial aspect, and totally passing by those moral and political considerations which make nations great, and by the influence of which alone men are distinguished from animals.

Well, what has been the result of this attempt during the reign of Liberalism for the disintegration of the Empire? It has entirely failed. But how has it failed? Through the sympathy of the Colonies with the Mother Country. They have decided that the Empire shall not be destroyed, and in my opinion no minister in this country will do his duty who neglects any opportunity of reconstructing as much as possible our Colonial Empire, and of responding to those distant sympathies which may become the source of incalculable strength and happiness to this land. Therefore, gentlemen, with respect to the second great object of the Tory party also — the maintenance of the Empire — public opinion appears to be in favour of our principles — that public opinion which, I am bound to say, thirty years ago, was not favourable to our principles, and which, during a long interval of controversy, in the interval had been doubtful . . .

Before sitting down, I would make one remark particularly

applicable to those whom I am now addressing . . . When you return to your homes, when you return to your counties and to your cities, you must tell to all those whom you can influence that the time is at hand, that, at least, it cannot be far distant, when England will have to decide between national and cosmopolitan principles. The issue is not a mean one. It is whether you will be content to be a comfortable England, modelled and moulded upon Continental principles and meeting in due course an inevitable fate, or whether you will be a great country, — an Imperial country, — a country where your sons, when they rise, rise to paramount positions, and obtain not merely the esteem of their countrymen, but command the respect of the world.

(T. E. Kebbel (ed.), *Selected Speeches of the late Right Honourable the Earl of Beaconsfield* (London, 1882), vol.II, 529–31, 534.)

DOCUMENT VIII   Disraeli's speech in the House of Commons on the second reading of the Royal Titles Bill, 9 March 1876

Disraeli announces the new royal title and attempts to answer some of the criticisms previously made by opponents.

I am empowered, therefore, to say that the title would be 'Empress,' and that Her Majesty would be 'Victoria, by the Grace of God, of the United Kingdom of Great Britain and Ireland, Queen, Defender of the Faith, and Empress of India.' Now, I know it may be said — it was said at a recent debate and urged strongly by the right. hon. Gentleman the Member for Bradford (Mr W. E. Forster) — that this addition to Her Majesty's style, and in this addition alone, we are treating without consideration the colonies. I cannot in any way concur in that opinion. No one honours more than myself the colonial Empire of England; no one is more anxious to maintain it. No one regrets more than I do that favourable opportunities have been lost of identifying the colonies with the Royal race of England. But we have to deal now with another subject, and one essentially different from the colonial condition. The condition of India and the condition of the colonies have no similarity. In the colonies you have, first of all, a fluctuating population — a man is Member of Parliament, it may be, for Melbourne this year, and next year he is a Member of Parliament for Westminster. A colonist finds a nugget, or he fleeces a thousand flocks. He makes a fortune, he returns to England, he buys an estate, he becomes a magistrate, he represents Majesty, he becomes High Sheriff; he has a magnificent house near Hyde Park; and he goes to Court, to levées, to drawing rooms; he has an opportunity of plighting his troth personally to his Sovereign, he is in frequent and direct communication with her. But that is not the case with the inhabitant of India. The condition of colonial society is of a fluctuating character. Its political and social elements change . . . There is no similarity between the circumstances of our colonial fellow-subjects and those of our fellow-subjects in India. Our colonists are English; they come, they go, they are careful to make fortunes, to invest their money in England; their interests in this country are immense, ramified, complicated, and they have constant opportunities of improving and enjoying the relations which exist between themselves and their countrymen in the metropolis. Their relations to the Sovereign are ample; they satisfy them, the colonists are proud of those relations, they are interested in the titles of the Queen, they look forward to return when they leave England, they do return — in short, they are Englishmen. Now let me say a word before I move the second reading of this Bill upon the effect it may have upon India. It is not without consideration, it is not without utmost care, it is not until after the deepest thought that we have thought it our duty to introduce this Bill into Parliament. It is desired in India. It is anxiously expected. The Princes and nations of India — unless we are deceived, and we have omitted no means by which we could obtain and form opinions — look to it with the utmost interest. They know exactly what it means, though there may be some hon. Members in this House who do not. They know in India what this Bill means, and they know what it means is what they wish. I do myself most earnestly impress upon the House to remove prejudice from their minds and to pass the second reading of this Bill, without a division. Let not our divisions be misconstrued. Let the people of India feel that there is a sympathetic chord between us and them; and do not let Europe suppose for a moment that there are any in this House who are not deeply conscious of the importance of our Indian Empire. Unfortunate words have been heard in the debate upon this subject. But I will not believe that any Member of this House seriously contemplated the loss of our Indian Empire. I trust, therefore, that the House will give to this Bill a second reading without a division. By the permission of the Queen I have communicated, on the part of my Colleagues, the intention of Her Majesty, which She will express in her Proclamation, if you sanction the passing of this Bill. It will be an act, to my mind, that will add splendour even to her Throne, and security even to her Empire.

(*Hansard's Parliamentary Debates,* Third series, vol. 227, cols. 1725–7.)

DOCUMENT IX   Edward Dicey's views on empire, September 1877

Edward Dicey, editor of the Observer, *challenges Gladstone's liberal views on empire.*

For my own part, I cannot honestly put forward the plea so often urged of late, and to which Mr Gladstone seems to have given the sanction of his high approval, that we rule India and other portions of our Empire, in which we are masters and not settlers, on account of the benefits we confer, or hope to confer, on the subject race. To my thinking it is a mere pretence to say that we went to India in the first instance, or stop there now, because we believe our presence to be a boon to the Hindoos . . . We too have followed our star, fulfilled our destiny, worked out the will implanted in us; and to say that we have been influenced in the main by any higher motive seems to me a self-deception. Still, though to assert that we have gone forth to foreign lands for the sake of doing good would be sheer hypocrisy, we may fairly say that we have done good by going, and are doing good by stopping. In the countries, such as Canada, Australia, and the Cape, where we have planted ourselves as settlers, the world at large has been the gainer by the substitution of civilisation for savagery . . . And with respect to countries like India or Ceylon, where we rule as masters, not as settlers, as conquerors rather than as emigrants, we can make out a fair defence for our supremacy. We have substituted law and order for anarchy and oppression, settled peace for intestine warfare, a higher standard of government for a lower . . . Whatever else we may have failed to do, the mere existence of our Empire has brought new life into lands stagnant for ages, has stirred up dormant energies, has instilled the rudimental ideas of individual liberty, equality before the law, and public duty . . .

For my own part, however, I must own that Mr Gladstone's whole theory as to our rule in India seems to me untenable. He asserts that

'we have no interest in India except the well-being of India itself';
and that we retain our rule of India, not for any profit or advantage
of our own, but simply because, having 'of our own motion wedded
the fortunes of that country, we could never in honour solicit a
divorce.' . . . I do not dispute for one moment that as a nation we do
honestly wish to benefit the natives of India. I believe sincerely that
our rule does benefit the natives. But, as a matter of fact, we rule
India, not because we wish to benefit the natives, still less because
the natives are conscious of the benefits we confer upon them, but
because we deem the possession of India conducive to our interests
and our reputation, because we have got it and intend to keep it,
because to us has been given a mission like to that of ancient Rome
. . . I am convinced that the nation is firm in its conviction that the
Empire of England must be upheld at all costs and all hazards.

(E. Dicey, 'Mr Gladstone and Our Empire', *The Nineteenth Century*,
September 1877, vol.II, 299–300, 305–6.)

DOCUMENT X   'By Jingo'

*The word 'jingoism' is derived from the famous music-hall song written by
G. W. Hunt in 1877 and performed by G. H. MacDermott during the crisis
of 1877–8.*

The 'Dogs of War' are loose and the rugged Russian Bear,
Full bent on blood and robbery, has crawled out of his lair,
It seems a thrashing now and then, will never help to tame,
The brute, and so he's bent upon the 'same old game'.
The Lion did his best to find him some excuse,
To crawl back to his den again, all efforts were no use,
He hunger'd for his victim, he's pleased when blood is shed,
But let us hope his crimes may all recoil on his own head.

As peacemaker old England her very utmost tried,
The Russians said they wanted peace but then those Russians lied.
Of carnage and of trickery, they'll have sufficient feast,
Ere they dare to think of coming near our road unto the east.
So we're waiting for the signal, directly up it runs
Clear the decks for action, stand by the guns;
Our army and our navy, true British dogs of war,
Will make them cry 'peccavi' [I have sinned] same as they did before.

Chorus: We don't want to fight,
But by jingo if we do,
We've got the ships, we've got the men,
We've got the money too,
We've fought the Bear before,
And while we're Britons true,
The Russians shall not have Constantinople.

DOCUMENT XI   Gladstone on England's Mission, September 1878

After the Congress of Berlin, Gladstone continued his onslaught on the government's foreign and imperial policies during the parliamentary recess by contributing an article to the journal The Nineteenth Century.

Territorial aggrandisement, backed by military display, is the *cheval de bataille* of the administration. Empire is greatness; leagues of land are empire; your safety is measured by the fear you strike into other nations; trade follows the flag; he that doubts is an enemy to his country. This creed of aggrandisement, made real to the public imagination by the acquisition of a Mediterranean and virtually European island [Cyprus], has operated a relative success . . . The Government, not uniformly nor consistently, but in the main and on the whole, have opened up and relied upon an illegitimate source of power, which never wholly fails: they have appealed, under the prostituted name of patriotism, to exaggerated fears, to imaginary interests, and to the acquisitiveness of a race which has surpassed every other known to history in the faculty of appropriating to itself vast spaces of the earth, and establishing its supremacy over men of every race and language. Now I hold to stimulate these tendencies, to overlook the proportion between our resources and our obligations, and above all to claim anything more than equality of rights in the moral and political intercourse of the world, is not the way to make England great, but to make it both morally and materially little.

The sentiment of empire may be called innate in every Briton. If there are exceptions, they are like those of men born blind or lame among us. It is part of our patrimony; born with our birth, dying only with our death; incorporating itself in the first elements of our knowledge, and interwoven with all our habits of mental action upon public affairs. It is a portion of our national stock, which has never been deficient, but which has more than once run to rank excess, and brought us to mischief accordingly, mischief that for a time we have weakly thought was ruin . . .

Between the two parties in this controversy there is a perfect agreement that England has a mighty mission in the world; but there is a discord as fundamental upon the question what that mission is.

I. With the one party, her first care is held to be the care of her own children within her own shores, the redress of wrongs, the supply of needs, the improvement of laws and institutions. Against this homespun doctrine, the present Government appears to set up territorial aggrandisement, large establishments, and the accumulation of a multitude of fictitious interests abroad, as if our real interests were not enough; and since the available store of national time and attention is a fixed quantity, there ensues that comparative remissness in domestic affairs, which is too conclusively shown by the beggarly returns to our legislation, the aggravation of our burdens, and the fast-growing arrears of business.

II. With the one party, the great duty and honour and charge of our transmarine Colonial Empire is, to rear up free congenital communities . . . It is the administrative connection, and the shadow of political subordination, which chiefly give them value in the sight of the party, who at home as well as abroad are striving to cajole or drive us into Imperialism . . .

. . . We do not want Bosnian submissions. Especially is it inexpedient to acquire possessions which, like Cyprus, never can become truly British, because they have acquired indelibly an ethnical character of their own. In them we remain as masters and as foreigners, and the connection at its best has not the ennobling features which, in cases like America and Australasia, give a high moral purpose to the subsisting relation, and compensate for the serious responsibilities which in given contingencies it may entail.

(W. E. Gladstone, 'England's Mission', *The Nineteenth Century*, September 1878, vol.IV, 568–73.)

DOCUMENT XII   Robert Lowe's attack on 'Imperialism', October 1878

Robert Lowe, former Liberal chancellor of the Exchequer, joins in the debate.

Let us examine this new idol to which we are summoned to bow down, as suddenly and as unreasonably as the subjects of Nebuchadnezzar himself. What does Imperialism mean? It means the assertion of absolute force over others. If we can gain some purpose by persuading our adversary that we are right and he is wrong, that is mere logical and rhetorical dexterity. There is nothing imperial in it. If we can, by abating somewhat of our extreme right, or even by larger concessions, avert the calamities of war, that is utterly repugnant to Imperialism. But if by the menace of overbearing force we can coerce a weaker state to bow before our will, or if, better still, we can by a demonstration of actual force attain the same object, or, best of all, if we can conquer our adversary in open fight, and impose our own conditions at the bayonet's point, then, as Dryden sings, 'these are imperial arts and worthy thee.' It does not follow that the strongest party is always in the wrong, but the triumph of Imperialism is most complete when power is most clearly manifested; and of course the victory is doubled when the victory is not only over weakness but over right.

We do not say that in her long and chequered history England has not often abused her power, but we believe that this is the first time that the leading members of her Government in England have descended so low as to teach their party to put forward such a symbol. Let us see what it is, and whither it will lead us. We are told as a matter of reproach that the question is between a great and a little England. Whether there may not also be a choice sometimes between a happy and a great, between an imperial and a just England, we are never desired to consider . . .

. . . We have yet to say a word on the influence of this pernicious innovation on our own constitution. Belial[1] is a divinity who will not be served by halves, and no nation ever cast away the principles of just and fair dealing in its relations with others, without speedily feeling the recoil in its domestic affairs. Of all countries in the world England is the one which affords the readiest opportunity for unscrupulous persons to practise the arts of Imperialism as we have explained the term. The history of the English constitution is a record of liberties wrung and extorted bit by bit from arbitrary power. The shell of absolute power has been allowed to remain, so much of substance being removed as the emergencies of a particular crisis rendered necessary. When the prerogatives of the Sovereign have been grossly abused, they have been restricted, but . . . most of the prerogatives of the Crown remain untouched, the country having been content with the assurance that they can only be exercised under the advice of responsible ministers.

It is the happy discovery of the present Parliament that responsibility has no terrors for a Government possessed of a large and manageable majority. Our institutions are framed in a spirit of generous but, as it now appears, mistaken confidence. The power of entering into treaties without the consent of Parliament has been only retained because it was believed that it would not be abused. That by the abuse of this power the members of the Cabinet, without consulting Parliament, should be able to pledge the country to the most formidable engagements, to the clandestine acquisition of new territory peculiarly calculated to wound the susceptibilities of powers with whom it is alike our desire and interest to be on the most amicable terms, and to a treaty under which we may be called upon at a moment's notice to engage under every conceivable disadvantage in a war in a desolate and remote country with one of the greatest military powers in the world, as near to his resources as we are distant from our own, can only be believed possible because it has just been actually done. It is thus that the poisoned chalice of Imperialism which we have held out to our allies and rivals is now commended to our lips. We have been learning under our present guides and leaders the doctrines of despotic and arbitrary power, and we must not repine if we experience in our own persons that which we are taught by these our new schoolmasters to be the proper treatment of our friends and allies. Thus it has ever been. The laws of good faith and fair dealing are violated towards strangers, in the vain hope that those virtues may flourish at home which are cynically cast aside abroad.

But this can never be. The spirit which teaches that the means are justified if the end be obtained, will not suffer its sphere of action to be limited to dealings with our adversaries or our allies. If all is held to be fair in war or diplomacy, it is but a slight step in advance to hold that political opponents within our own borders are entitled to no greater consideration . . . The people should be put on their guard against the flimsy but dangerous delusions to which they are exposed . . . They should be guarded against those odious sophisms which, under the vulgar mask of Imperialism, conceal the substitution of might for right, and seek to establish the dominion of one set of human beings on the degradation and misery of another. And above all, the public ought to be warned against that abuse of the prerogative of making treaties, by which, in defiance of constitutional practice and theory, we have been entangled in the most tremendous liabilities without the previous consent of the Parliament that should have sanctioned, or the people who must bear them.

(Robert Lowe, 'Imperialism', *Fortnightly Review*, October 1878, vol.XXIV, 458–9, 463–4.)

1. The spirit of evil personified (i.e. the devil).

DOCUMENT XIII Carnarvon's address on imperial administration to the Philosophical Institution, Edinburgh, 5 November 1878

The earl of Carnarvon, no longer a member of the Cabinet, attempts to identify a true and a false imperialism.

We have been much perplexed by a new word, 'Imperialism,' which has crept in among us . . . I have heard of Imperial policy, and Imperial interests, but Imperialism, as such, is a newly coined word to me . . .

I believe there is a true and a false Imperialism. But, what is the true and what the false? We can, perhaps, best tell what Imperialism is by ascertaining what it is not. It is certainly not Caesarism. It is not that base second-hand copy of Continental despotism — that bastard monarchy begotten in the slime of political and financial corruption. It has nothing in common with that . . . Nor, again, has Imperialism in the true sense of the word any connection with what has been called 'personal government.' Our Constitution is clear on that point. We know that the Crown has certain prerogatives, and that Parliament has certain rights and duties, but that neither Parliament nor the Crown may act alone . . . Nor is Imperialism, again, mere bulk of territory and multiplication of subjects. We sometimes hear the words, 'A great England and a little England,' but we do not measure nations by their size or numbers, any more than we measure men by their inches . . .

One word more as to foreign Imperialism. Thank God we have nothing to copy there. Foreign Imperialism means vast standing armies; and at this moment we have before our eyes the nations of Europe divided into hostile and suspicious camps . . . But if we turn our eyes from that gloomy spectacle to the great Empire of England, we see, at all events for the present, a brighter and more peaceful picture in the self-government of the great Anglo-Saxon Colonies. Here lies the true strength of our Imperialism . . . 'These are Imperial Arts, and worthy Thee', it may truly be said; — and though at this moment the future prospects of the world may seem to some to be overclouded, we may cherish the hope that as time goes on the common instincts of language, faith, laws, institutions, of allegiance to a common sovereign, may draw the bonds between them and us yet closer. We should be indeed closely wedded to the dull prose of daily life if we banished wholly from our imagination that noble dream, which may yet in the fullness of time be realised, of a great English-speaking community, united together in a peaceful confederation, too powerful to be molested by any nation, and too powerful and too generous, I hope, to molest any weaker State.

Or, again, if we turn to that far larger empire over our native fellow-subjects of which I have spoken, the limits expand and the proportions rise, till there forms itself a picture so vast and noble that the mind loses itself in the contemplation of what might be under the beneficent rule of England if faction could be still and selfish ambition be held back, and rest from war and war's exhausting burdens could be given. There we have races struggling to emerge into civilisation, to whom emancipation from servitude is but the foretaste of the far higher law of liberty and progress to which they may yet attain, and vast populations like those of India sitting like children in the shadow of doubt and poverty and sorrow, yet looking up to us for guidance and for help. To them it is our part to give wise laws, good government, and a well-ordered finance, which is the foundation of good things in human communities; it is ours to provide them with a system where the humblest may enjoy freedom from oppression and wrong equally with the greatest; where the light of morality and religion can penetrate into the darkest dwelling-places. This is the real fulfilment of our duties; this, again I say, is the true strength and meaning of imperialism.

(Earl of Carnarvon, 'Imperial Administration', *Fortnightly Review*, December 1878, vol.XXIV, 760–1, 763–4.)

DOCUMENT XIV   Gladstone's Midlothian Campaign: Glasgow, 5 December 1879

Gladstone, nearing the end of his first Midlothian campaign, denounces

*Beaconsfield's foreign and imperial policies before an audience of nearly
6,000 people in St Andrew's Hall, Glasgow.*

Now I want to say a word, if you will allow me, upon this safe-
guarding of the road to India. I want to know what is the meaning of
that claim. In the principles of foreign policy, gentlemen, as I have
professed them from my youth, it is a fundamental article that we are
to set up no claim for ourselves which we do not allow to others, and
that he who departs from that principle is committing treason
against public law and the peace and order of the world. What is the
meaning of safe-guarding the road to India? It seems to mean this;
that a little island at one end of the world, having possessed itself of
an enormous territory at the other end of the world, is entitled to say
with respect to every land and every sea lying between its own shores
and any part of that enormous possession, that it has a preferential
right to the possession or control of that intermediate territory, in
order, as it is called, to safe-guard the road to India. That,
gentlemen, is a monstrous claim.

. . . It seems to me, gentlemen, that for the last two years we have
been under what calls itself a policy; but it is no policy. It is what is
better known by an outlandish term, yet one not inapplicable — it is
a phantasmagoria. We have gone up into the mountains; we have
broken Afghanistan to pieces; we have driven mothers and children
forth from their homes to perish in the snow; we have spent a
treasure, of which a real account has never yet been rendered; we
have undergone an expenditure of which as yet I believe we are
aware but a fraction; we have renewed and redoubled the wrong
which our fathers did to Afghanistan forty years ago . . . Sher Ali[1]
whom we have sent in sorrow to his grave, endeavoured at times, as
civilised Powers too will do, to make the most of his connection with
us. But he never committed an offence against us; he never gave us
the slightest cause even for distrust of his ultimate intentions. It was
our wilful action, and our wilful action alone, that raised the cause of
quarrel. And, gentlemen, what is true of Cyprus on a small scale, is
true of Afghanistan on a greater scale. The fact that the result of our
enterprise is nothing to ourselves but mischief and embarrassment,
does not in the slightest degree redeem us from the charge of a guilty
cupidity under which that enterprise was undertaken.

. . . In Africa you have before you the memory of bloodshed, of
military disaster, the record of 10,000 Zulus — such is the
computation of Bishop Colenso[2] — slain for no other offence than

their attempt to defend against your artillery with their naked bodies their hearths and homes, their wives and families. You have the invasion of a free people in the Transvaal; and you have, I fear, in one quarter or another, — I will not enter into details, which might be injurious to the public interest, — prospects of further disturbance and shedding of blood. You have an Afghanistan ruined; you have India not advanced, but thrown back in government, subjected to heavy and unjust charges, subjected to what may well be termed, in comparison with the mild government of former years, a system of oppression; and with all this you have had at home, in matters I will not detail, the law broken, and the rights of Parliament invaded. Gentlemen, amidst the whole of this pestilent activity, — for so I must call it, — this distress and bloodshed which we have either produced or largely shared in producing, not in one instance down to the Treaty of Berlin, and down to the war in Afghanistan, — not in one instance did we either do a deed, or speak an effectual word, on behalf of liberty. Such is the upshot, gentlemen, of the sad enumeration. To call this policy Conservative is, in my opinion, a pure mockery, and an abuse of terms. Whatever it may be in its motive, it is in its result disloyal, it is in its essence thoroughly subversive . . . Gentlemen, I wish to end as I began. Is this the way, or is this not the way, in which a free nation, inhabiting these islands, wishes to be governed? Will the people, be it now or be it months hence, ratify the deeds that have been done, and assume upon themselves that tremendous responsibility? The whole humble aim, gentlemen, of my proceedings has been to bring home, as far as was in my power, this great question to the mind and to the conscience of the community at large.

(W. E. Gladstone, *Political Speeches in Scotland, November and December 1879* (London, 1879), 196, 204–5, 209–10.)

1. Sher Ali, amir of Afghanistan.
2. John William Colenso, bishop of Natal.

Bibliography

There are numerous textbooks which provide a good introduction to the period covered by the present study. These include: Norman McCord, *British History, 1815–1906* (Oxford, Oxford University Press, 1991); Michael Bentley, *Politics without Democracy, 1815–1914: Perception and Preoccupation in British Government* (London, Fontana, 1984); Norman Gash, *Aristocracy and the People: Britain 1815–1865* (London, Edward Arnold, 1979); Richard Shannon, *The Crisis of Imperialism, 1865–1915* (London, Hart-Davis, MacGibbon, 1976); E. J. Feuchtwanger, *Democracy and Empire: Britain, 1865–1914* (London, Edward Arnold, 1985); and Donald Read, *The Age of Urban Democracy: England, 1868–1914* (rev. edn, London, Longman, 1994). A brief but splendid overview of the later period is to be found in Paul Adelman, *Gladstone, Disraeli and Later Victorian Politics* (2nd edn, London, Longman, 1983).

Biographies of Disraeli are legion, varying in length, praise and condemnation. The most balanced and scholarly biography is Robert (later Lord) Blake, *Disraeli* (London, Eyre & Spottiswoode, 1966), though this needs to be supplemented by more recently published material. It rests heavily on the 'official' biography by W. F. Monypenny and G.E. Buckle, *The Life of Benjamin Disraeli, Earl of Beaconsfield* (6 vols., London, John Murray, 1910–20), a monumental work, favourable to its subject, which contains such a vast amount of correspondence and other documentary evidence that it remains indispensable. Another good biography, especially on personal details, is Sarah Bradford, *Disraeli* (London, Weidenfeld & Nicholson, 1982). The most recent biography by Stanley Weintraub, *Disraeli: A Biography* (London, Hamish Hamilton, 1993), is most likely to be remembered for the suggestion that Disraeli may have fathered one or two illegitimate children. There are good accounts of Disraeli's career in J. T. Ward, 'Derby and Disraeli', in Donald Southgate (ed.), *The Conservative Leadership, 1832–1932* (London, Macmillan, 1974), 58–100, and John Vincent, 'Disraeli', in H. Van

Thal (ed.), *The Prime Ministers* (2 vols., London, Allen & Unwin, 1975), II, 85–108.

Two helpful introductions are the excellent 'Lancaster Pamphlet' by John Walton, *Disraeli* (London, Routledge, 1990) which has an important chapter on 'Nation and Empire', and (the fuller and more critical) Ian Machin, *Disraeli* (London, Longman, 1995). John Vincent's *Disraeli* (Oxford, Oxford University Press, 1990) is an interesting examination of Disraeli's thought, including his fictional writings. This may be complemented by W. Stafford, 'Romantic élitism in the thought of Benjamin Disraeli', *Literature and History*, 6 (1980), 43–58.

Standard works on various aspects of Disraeli's career include: F. B. Smith, *The Making of the Second Reform Bill* (Cambridge, Cambridge University Press, 1966); Maurice Cowling, *1867: Disraeli, Gladstone and Revolution — the Passing of the Second Reform Bill* (Cambridge, Cambridge University Press, 1967); Paul Smith, *Disraelian Conservatism and Social Reform* (London, Routledge, 1967); and E. J. Feuchtwanger, *Disraeli, Democracy and the Tory Party: Conservative Leadership and Organisation after the Second Reform Act* (Oxford, Clarendon Press, 1968). For the financial aspect of Disraeli's career, see P. R. Ghosh, 'Disraelian Conservatism: a financial approach', *English Historical Review*, 99 (1984), 268–96, which ranges more widely than its title suggests, and H. C. G. Matthew, 'Disraeli, Gladstone and the politics of mid-Victorian budgets', *Historical Journal*, 22 (1979), 615–43.

Three very useful discussions of Disraeli's principles and the consistency with which he adhered to them, are to be found in: C. J. Lewis, 'Theory *versus* expediency in the policy of Disraeli', *Victorian Studies*, 4 (1961), 237–58; Paul Smith, 'Disraeli's politics', *Transactions of the Royal Historical Society*, 37 (1987), 65–85; and P. R. Ghosh, 'Style and substance in Disraelian social reform, *c.* 1860–80', in P. J. Waller (ed.), *Politics and Social Change in Modern Britain: Essays presented to A. F. Thompson* (Hassocks, Harvester Press, 1987), 59–90.

For placing Disraeli in his Conservative party context, the following works are indispensable: Robert M. Stewart, *The Foundation of the Conservative Party, 1830–67* (London, Longman, 1978) and Richard Shannon, *The Age of Disraeli, 1868–81: The Rise of Tory Democracy* (London, Longman, 1992). The latter is a particularly detailed, well-rounded and up-to-date account. Also useful are Lord Blake, *The Conservative Party from Peel to Thatcher*

(London, Methuen, 1985) and Bruce Coleman, *Conservatism and the Conservative Party in Nineteenth-century Britain* (London, Edward Arnold, 1988). An older work still worth consulting is H. J. Hanham, *Elections and Party Management. Politics in the Time of Disraeli and Gladstone* (London, Longman, 1959). (See also, W. D. McIntyre, 'Disraeli's election blunder: the Straits of Malacca issue in the 1874 election', *Renaissance and Modern Studies*, 5 (1961), 76–105.) Contemporary accounts of Disraeli's second administration are to be found in G. C. Thompson, *Public Opinion and Lord Beaconsfield, 1875–1880* (2 vols., London, Macmillan, 1886) and P. W. Clayden, *England under Lord Beaconsfield: The Political History of Six Years from the End of 1873 to the Beginning of 1880* (London, Kegan Paul, 1880; reprinted 1971). The latter is a rather jaundiced account.

The most useful brief introduction to the nineteenth-century empire is probably Frank McDonough, *The British Empire, 1815–1914* (London, Hodder & Stoughton, 1994). Three more detailed accounts are: Bernard Porter, *The Lion's Share: A Short History of British Imperialism, 1850–1983* (2nd edn, London, Longman, 1985); Ronald Hyam, *Britain's Imperial Century, 1815–1914: A Study of Empire and Expansion* (rev. edn, London, Macmillan, 1992); and C. C. Eldridge, *Victorian Imperialism* (London, Hodder & Stoughton, 1978). There are also useful essays in C. C. Eldridge (ed.), *British Imperialism in the Nineteenth Century* (London, Macmillan, 1984). On the 'New Imperialism', an excellent brief introduction by Andrew Porter, *European Imperialism, 1860–1914* (Basingstoke, Macmillan, 1994), should be consulted.

The two most frequently cited works on the empire in the age of Disraeli and Gladstone are W. D. McIntyre, *The Imperial Frontier in the Tropics, 1865–75: A Study of British Colonial Policy in West Africa, Malaya and the South Pacific in the Age of Gladstone and Disraeli* (London, Macmillan, 1967), and C. C. Eldridge, *England's Mission: The Imperial Idea in the Age of Gladstone and Disraeli, 1868–80* (London, Macmillan, 1973). The period is also covered in S. R. Stembridge, *Parliament, the Press and the Colonies, 1846–80* (New York, Garland, 1982) — a somewhat disappointing book as the work of an early Ph.D. seems not to have been updated — and P. J. Durrans, 'The House of Commons and the British Empire, 1868–1880', *Canadian Journal of History*, 9 (1974), 19–44. Freda Harcourt has contributed an article on 'Gladstone, monarchism and the "New Imperialism", 1868–74', *Journal of Imperial and Commonwealth History*, 14 (1985), 20–51, which complements her article on Disraeli. The problem of imperial defence is reviewed in D. C. Gordon, *The Dominion Partnership in Imperial Defense, 1870–1914* (Baltimore, John Hopkins Press, 1965).

While Disraeli's views on colonies and the empire are frequently referred to in monographs, comparatively little research has been done on this subject. The most influential contributions, cited in the first chapter of this book, are:

J. L. Morison, 'The Imperial Ideas of Benjamin Disraeli', *Canadian Historical Review*, 1 (1920), 267–80. A highly critical response to the publication of the final volume of the official biography.

C. A. Bodelsen, *Studies in Mid-Victorian Imperialism* (London, Heinemann, 1924; reprinted New York, Fertig, 1960). A dated, but still useful, examination of mid-Victorian attitudes which established the 'orthodox' interpretation of Disraeli's policy and attitudes towards empire.

Richard Koebner and Helmut D. Schmidt, *Imperialism: The Story and Significance of a Political Word, 1840–1960* (Cambridge, Cambridge University Press, 1964). While still set in the older mould of a great divide in imperial history about 1870, the authors reassess the significance of Disraeli's Crystal Palace speech, trace the development of Disraeli's imperial ideas during the Royal Titles controversy and the Eastern Question crisis, and plot the emergence of 'imperialism' as a hostile slogan in party strife by 1880.

S. R. Stembridge, 'Disraeli and the millstones', *Journal of British Studies*, 5 (1965), 122–39. By far the best general overview of Disraeli's policies and attitudes towards empire; a crucial article in the historiography of Disraeli's imperial ideas.

C. F. Goodfellow, *Great Britain and South African Confederation, 1870–81* (Cape Town, Oxford University Press, 1966). The fullest account of Carnarvon's confederation scheme, his role in the annexation of the Transvaal and the events leading to the Zulu war.

W. D. McIntyre, *The Imperial Frontier in the Tropics, 1865–75* (listed above), discusses, and disposes of, the idea that the Conservatives expanded the empire according to a new Conservative philosophy of empire in a series of planned 'forward movements'.

Maurice Cowling, 'Lytton, the Cabinet and the Russians, August to November, 1878', *English Historical Review*, 76 (1961), 59–79, attempts to demonstrate that Lord Lytton, a rebellious pro-consul, was responsible for causing the second Afghan war.

Ira Klein, 'Who made the Second Afghan War?', *Journal of Asian History*, 8 (1974), 97–121, shows that Cranbrook, Disraeli and the cabinet must bear a large part of the responsibility for the Afghan war.

Freda M. Harcourt, 'Disraeli's Imperialism, 1866–8: a question of timing', *Historical Journal*, 23 (1980), 87–109, suggests Disraeli launched the New Imperialism in 1867 for domestic reasons.

Nini Rodgers, 'The Abyssinian expedition of 1867–8: Disraeli's imperialism or James Murray's war?', *Historical Journal*, 27 (1984), 129–49, after a detailed examination of the origins of the war criticizes Harcourt's thesis.

Peter J. Durrans, 'A two-edged sword: the Liberal attack on Disraelian imperialism', *Journal of Imperial and Commonwealth History*, 10 (1982), 262–84. An excellent analysis of the Liberal attack on Disraeli's foreign and imperial policies, 1876–80.

Most writing on Disraeli's colonial policy has focused on the years 1874–80. McIntyre's book, *The Imperial Frontier in the Tropics,* covers West Africa, the South Pacific and the Malay States. Other works worth consulting are: R. E. Dummett, 'Pressure groups, bureaucracy and the decision-making process: the case of slavery abolition and colonial expansion in the Gold Coast, 1874', *Journal of Imperial and Commonwealth History*, 9 (1981), 193–215; D. Routledge, 'The negotiations leading to the cession of Fiji', *Journal of Imperial and Commonwealth History*, 2 (1974), 278–93; D. Scarr, *Fragments of Empire: A History of the Western Pacific High Commission, 1877–1919* (Canberra, Australian National University Press, 1980); and D. R. Sar Desai. 'The resident system in Malaya, 1874–1878', *Journal of the Historical Society of the University of Malaya*, 3 (1964–5), 94–106.

On South Africa, Goodfellow's *Great Britain and South African*

Confederation, the fullest account of Carnarvon's confederation scheme, lacks an economic dimension and therefore needs to be supplemented by: D. Welsh, *The Roots of Segregation: Native Policy in Colonial Natal, 1845–1910* (Cape Town, Oxford University Press, 1971); A. Atmore and S. Marks, 'The imperial factor in South Africa in the nineteenth century: towards a reassessment', *Journal of Imperial and Commonwealth History*, 3 (1974), 105–39; Norman Etherington, 'Labour supply and the genesis of South African confederation in the 1870s', *Journal of African History*, 20 (1979), 235–53; and R. L. Cope, 'Local imperative and imperial policy: the sources of Lord Carnarvon's South African confederation policy', *International Journal of African Historical Studies*, 20 (1987), 601–26. To C. A. Uys, *In the Era of Shepstone: British Expansion in South Africa, 1842–77* (Lovedale, Lovedale Press, 1933) needs to be added R. L. Cope, 'Shepstone, the Zulus and the annexation of the Transvaal', *South African Historical Journal*, 4 (1972), 45–63, and J. E. Yarett, 'The British annexation of the Transvaal', *Historia*, 19 (1974), 46–59. British policy and the origins of the Zulu war may be traced in the biography of Hicks Beach (listed below); J. Martineau, *Life and Correspondence of Sir Bartle Frere* (2 vols., London, Murray, 1895); W. B. Worsfold, *Sir Bartle Frere: A Footnote to the History of the British Empire* (London, Thornton Butterworth, 1923); and A. Duminy and C. Ballard, *The Anglo-Zulu War: New Perspectives* (Pietermaritzburg, University of Natal Press, 1981). By far the best modern treatment of the Zulu war is Ian J. Knight, *Brave Men's Blood* (London, Greenhill, 1990).

Conservative policy towards India is covered in S. Gopal, *British Policy in India, 1858–1905* (Cambridge, Cambridge University Press, 1965); B. Prasad, *The Foundations of India's Foreign Policy, 1860–1882* (2 vols., Calcutta, Orient Longmans, 1955); Edward C. Moulton, *Lord Northbrook's Indian Administration, 1872–1876* (Bombay, Asia Publishing House, 1968); and Lady Elizabeth Balfour, *The History of Lord Lytton's Indian Administration, 1876 to 1880* (London, Longmans, Green, 1899). The latter is a highly partisan account. Making the Queen 'Empress of India' and the invention of the accompanying ceremonial is discussed in L. A. Knight, 'The Royal Titles Act and India', *Historical Journal*, 11 (1968), 488–507, and B. S. Cohn, 'Representing authority in Victorian India', in E. J. Hobsbawm and T. Ranger, (eds.), *The Invention of Tradition* (Cambridge, Cambridge University Press, 1984). There are numerous studies of India's relations with Afghanistan. The best are: W. Fraser-

Tytler, *Afghanistan: A Study of Political Developments in Central and Southern Asia* (2nd edn, London, Oxford University Press, 1953); D. K. Ghose, *England and Afghanistan: A Phase in their Relations* (Calcutta, World Press, 1960); J. L. Duthie, 'Some further insights into the working of mid-Victorian imperialism: Lord Salisbury, the 'forward' group and Anglo-Afghan relations, 1874–1878', *Journal of Imperial and Commonwealth History*, 8 (1980), 181–208; and D. P. Singhal, *India and Afghanistan, 1876–1907: A Study in Diplomatic Relations* (Brisbane, University of Queensland Press, 1963). Besides the two articles by Cowling and Klein on the events leading up to the Anglo-Afghan war, J. L. Duthie, 'Pragmatic diplomacy or imperial encroachment?: British policy towards Afghanistan, 1874–1879', *International History Review*, 5 (1983), 475–95, and B. Robson, *The Road to Kabul: The Second Afghan War, 1878–1881* (London, Arms & Armour Press, 1986) should also be consulted.

Study of foreign affairs can be approached most accessibly via an engaging short study by Muriel Chamberlain, *'Pax Britannica'? British Foreign Policy, 1789–1914* (London, Longman, 1988). Bernard Porter, *Britain, Europe and the World, 1850–1986: Delusions of Grandeur* (London, Allen & Unwin, 1987) gives a longer overview. Particularly useful in linking external and domestic affairs is Marvin Swartz, *The Politics of British Foreign Policy in the Era of Disraeli and Gladstone* (New York, St Martin's Press, 1985). The standard authorities on the Eastern Question are: R. W. Seton-Watson, *Disraeli, Gladstone and the Eastern Question* (London, Macmillan, 1935); R. Millman, *Britain and the Eastern Question, 1875–78* (Oxford, Clarendon Press, 1979); R. Shannon, *Gladstone and the Bulgarian Agitation, 1876* (London, Thomas Nelson & Sons, 1963); and W. N. Medlicott, *The Congress of Berlin and After: A Diplomatic History of the Near Eastern Settlement, 1878–1880* (2nd edn, London, Cass, 1938). Disraeli's role in the occupation of Cyprus is examined in D. Lee, *Great Britain and the Cyprus Convention of 1878* (Cambridge, Mass., Harvard University Press, 1934).

The final climax, the attack on 'Beaconsfieldism', deserves separate treatment. The most illuminating account is the article by P. J. Durrans in the *Journal of Imperial and Commonwealth History* for 1982 cited earlier. To this should be added his article on 'Beaconsfieldism' in C. C. Eldridge (ed.), *Empire, Politics and Popular Culture* (Lampeter, Trivium Publications no. 24, 1989). J. V. Crangle has an interesting article on 'The issue of imperialism in the Liberal campaign of 1880' in the *Indian Political Science Review*, 8 (1974),

41–54. Gladstone's *Midlothian Speeches, 1879* are available, with an introduction by M. R. D. Foot, in a reprint by Leicester University Press, 1971. Thoughtful analyses of this unusual campaign are to be found in N. D. Boyd, 'Gladstone, Midlothian and stump oratory', *Central States Speech Journal*, 30 (1979), 144–55, and Robert Kelley, 'Midlothian: a study in politics and ideas', *Victorian Studies*, 4 (1960), 119–40. On the difficult subject of jingoism and the Conservative attempt to hijack the language of patriotism, a convincing analysis is provided in three works by Hugh Cunningham: 'Jingoism in 1877–78', *Victorian Studies*, 14 (1971), 429–53; 'The language of patriotism, 1750–1914', *History Workshop Journal*, 12 (1981), 8–33; and 'The Conservative Party and patriotism', in R. Colls and P. Dodd (eds.), *Englishness: Politics and Culture, 1880–1920* (London, Croom Helm, 1986).

Finally, a word on sources. A wealth of material for understanding Disraeli's views on empire is to be found in Monypenny's and Buckle's 'official' biography and in the pages of *Hansard's Parliamentary Debates*. S. R. Stembridge relied heavily on these volumes for his 1965 article. An important new source, currently in progress, is the publication of Disraeli's letters, with other associated material. The volumes so far published include: J. A. W. Gunn, J. Matthews, D. M. Schurman and M. G. Wiebe (eds.), *Benjamin Disraeli: Letters*, vol. 1 (1815–34) and vol. 2 (1835–7) (Toronto, University of Toronto Press, 1982); J. A. W. Gunn, J. B. Conacher, J. Matthews and Mary S. Millar (eds.), *Benjamin Disraeli: Letters*, vol. 3 (1838–41) (Toronto, University of Toronto Press, 1987) and vol. 4 (1842–7) (Toronto, University of Toronto Press, 1989); and M. G. Wiebe, J. B. Conacher and J. Matthews (eds.), *Benjamin Disraeli: Letters*, vol. 5 (1848–51) (Toronto, University of Toronto Press, 1993). Disraeli's pamphlets and much of his early journalism are collected in William Hutcheon (ed.), *Whigs and Whiggism: Political Writings by Benjamin Disraeli* (London, John Murray, 1913). T. E. Kebbel, *Selected Speeches of the Late Right Honourable Earl of Beaconsfield* (2 vols., London, Longmans, Green, 1882) provides a good selection of Disraeli's parliamentary speeches on colonial, Indian and Irish matters and also on foreign affairs. The Marquis of Zetland (ed.), *The Letters of Disraeli to Lady Bradford and Lady Chesterfield* (2 vols., London, Ernest Benn, 1929) contains much gossip but also useful political insights.

In addition, biographies and journals of colleagues should be consulted. Among the most rewarding are: John Vincent (ed.), *Disraeli, Derby and the Conservative Party: Journals and Memoirs of Edward Henry, Lord Stanley* (Hassocks, Harvester Press, 1978); John Vincent (ed.), *A Selection from the Diaries of Edward Henry Stanley, 15th Earl of Derby (1826–93) Between September 1869 and March 1878*, Camden Fifth Series, vol. 4 (London, Royal Historical Society, 1994); Arthur Hardinge, *Life of Henry Howard Molyneaux Herbert, Fourth Earl of Carnarvon, 1831–1890* (3 vols., London, Humphrey Milford, Oxford University Press, 1925); A. E. Gathorne-Hardy, *Gathorne-Hardy, First Earl of Cranbrook: A Memoir with Extracts from His Diary and Correspondence* (2 vols., London, Longmans, Green, 1910); Nancy E. Johnson (ed.), *The Diary of Gathorne-Hardy, later Lord Cranbrook, 1866–1892: Political Selections* (Oxford, Oxford University Press, 1981); Lady Victoria Hicks Beach, *Life of Sir Michael Hicks Beach (Earl St Aldwyn)* (2 vols., London, Macmillan, 1932); Andrew Lang, *Life, Letters and Diaries of Sir Stafford Northcote, First Earl of Iddesleigh* (Edinburgh, Blackwood, 1890); and Lady Gwendolen Cecil, *Life of Robert, Marquis of Salisbury* (4 vols., London, Hodder & Stoughton, 1921–32).

Appendix: The Conservative Ministries, 1852–1880

February–December 1852:

Prime Minister	The fourteenth Earl of Derby
Foreign Secretary	Earl of Malmesbury
Secretary for War and the Colonies	Sir John Pakington
Chancellor of the Exchequer	Benjamin Disraeli

February–June 1858:

Prime Minister	The fourteenth Earl of Derby
Foreign Secretary	Earl of Malmesbury
Colonial Secretary	Lord Stanley
War Secretary	General Peel
Chancellor of the Exchequer	Benjamin Disraeli

June 1866–February 1867:

Prime Minister	The fourteenth Earl of Derby
Foreign Secretary	Lord Stanley
Colonial Secretary	Earl of Carnarvon
War Secretary	General Peel
Indian Secretary	Viscount Cranborne
Chancellor of the Exchequer	Benjamin Disraeli

February 1867–November 1868:

Prime Minister	Benjamin Disraeli
Foreign Secretary	Lord Stanley
Colonial Secretary	Duke of Buckingham

War Secretary	Sir John Pakington
Indian Secretary	Sir Stafford Northcote
Chancellor of the Exchequer	G. Ward Hunt

February 1874–April 1880:

Prime Minister	Benjamin Disraeli
Foreign Secretary	The fifteenth Earl of Derby
Colonial Secretary	Earl of Carnarvon
War Secretary	Gathorne Hardy
Indian Secretary	Marquis of Salisbury
Chancellor of the Exchequer	Sir Stafford Northcote

(In 1878, Derby and Carnarvon resigned. As a result, the Marquis of Salisbury became Foreign Secretary, Sir Michael Hicks Beach became Colonial Secretary, and Earl Cranbrook (Gathorne Hardy) became Indian Secretary.)

Index

Index of Historians Cited in the Text